Listening to this Life
by
Frank Lowe
ISBN: 978-1-9161066-2-8

PUBLISHING

i2i Publishing, Manchester.
www.i2ipublishing.co.uk

The Illustrations in this book are all from the pen of BazzMac

Contents

Foreword

I didn't want to stop, however, someone stood on the brakes, I skidded and lost control for a while, couldn't see which direction I was heading. Then, when I thought I had corrected matters I veered off course without anyone to check my compass or direction, I was in no-man's-land.

That's roughly where I stayed for several years. I was now my own navigator, engineer and captain of this rather confused ship of mine. The passengers – my family – who had to endure this journey kept telling me to find a port, stop, re-group, take a break and I would then see things differently.

Well this captain thought he could do his own thing, without any help or charts of where he was heading. In fact, he had no idea where he was taking himself and these totally innocent and loyal passengers.

It has been a while however, I am now moored in a better place and can at least gather some thoughts together of what comes next. Certainly not the world I knew and was forced to leave behind, that really was a danger zone riddled with human land 'minds'.

The problem is this, the new world I experience daily, in person on the street, hear on the radio - God save me from Nicky Campbell, or the mindless trash on terrestrial TV that is not for me either. If there is a parallel universe, then I might sign up for the journey right now.

You don't get a hand book when you become a parent nor a guide book on reaching a certain age, so what do you do? If one is normal and I believe I can reasonably fit that description, then all sorts of pursuits, hobbies and holidays are available to while away whatever time you have. That certainly didn't appeal, life had changed, and I was trying to come to terms with my new situation.

The conventions that I was having in my head were world class and destructive, every one of the demands was able to have a piece of me as and when they wanted, day or night. In fact, the night time visitors were easier to deal with. When the wolves began to circle, at least I could curse them out loud in the privacy of my home. Not so with the tormentors who came in the daytime. It was bad form to shout out loud at an imaginary foe in a crowded coffee shop, although that was exactly what I wanted to do and relieve the pressure.

So, for me to achieve some clarity of thought I had to, *leap off the carrousel, step outside my comfort zone, be kinder to myself and those around me, even forget myself for a while.* Someone else told me to *break the circle.* All great advice but not easy when you are the one taking it. You may even recognise that feeling.

Therefore, to get back on course I commit to paper that which seems to offer a distraction and which I find strangely therapeutic, my observations on human nature. How we all seem to bugger along as though life will go on as usual and assume nasty things happen to other people. In writing these short episodes I have, I admit, had to engage in a certain amount of voyeurism both at home and abroad. So, my apologies to all those folk who might have thought I was eves-dropping on their conversations. I couldn't help it, you were broadcasting to the nation!

Finally, with a little help from my GP, my Welsh friend Di Azipam and his mate Flo Oxytine, I may be able to navigate myself through these unchartered waters of anxiety however, its early days.

I hope you enjoy the rest.

Dedicated to Moi, Ben, Emily, Barbara, Denis, Di, Flo and Maggie.

If you share some of Frank Lowe's views about the world in general and coffee in particular, he would be delighted to hear from you on: -

frank520lowe@btinternet.com

Book One - Caffeine

1. 'Little Darlings'

"So, that's one large Mocha and a Baby Cheeno for your daughter." These were the words I overheard from the Barista taking an order from the young mother at the counter.
She continued, "How old is she now?"

"Just two," replied mother. Tailored faux fur coat, designer blue jeans and a classical pair of red boots, wow, impressive. Her mother was dressed in a similar outfit.

Now I've heard of a Chewelah and Shiatzu, however a baby Cheeno? That puzzled me, why would you order a puppy from a coffee shop?

"Double shot?" enquired the Barista, to which the mother nodded eagerly.

Mother turning to the little darling and asked in that language that only new parents and grandparents understand, "Chocolate sprinkles darling?"

It must have registered as the look on the infant's face was that of Christmas and her birthday arriving together. "Yeah!" came the piercing reply. Big smile and job done, one high octane shot of coffee and an injection of sugar for the little one.

Was I really witnessing the grooming of the next generation of caffeine junkies? What next, breast feeding latte? Was this to be a future where new mothers would become walking coffee machines passing on the caffeine directly to their off-spring, left for mocha or right for espresso?

A quick ready reckoner on costs and I predicted that over the next forty years this two-year-old, assuming she lives that long and the habit 'kicks in' would spend approximately £31,000, without taking inflation into account. Working on five cups per week at £3 per shot, over fifty-two weeks and by forty years. Now you can assume different criteria, however, this is a tidy sum. Alternatively, half that amount could buy her a face lift and neck tuck when she reaches twenty.

To complete the scene, the mother and toddler join a group of their peers where juniors are about to experiencing a collective 'baby high.' So much for a quiet afternoon for these mums and dads, soon the little darlings would be bouncing off the walls.

And so, it came to pass the effect of the caffeine first started to show when the activity level of the young ones, aged from approximately two to five years of age, began to 'run amock.' Thus, turning the relatively quiet recluse of a coffee shop into a playground without rules or parental guidance.

The excited group of parents were now in deep conversation about the latest episodes of 'Cheshire Housewives' and the 'Big Brother House.' This group debate was interrupted when one of the more adventurous children ran towards the glass fronted door to the café and smack, a full-on face contact. At first there was an absolute silence, next the child started to go a bright red, apart from the cheek which was by now white with the motif of the coffee shop firmly imprinted with a huge letter N. What followed can only be described as a cry from hell as the little darling let rip with a scream that would test the hitherto shatter-proof glass he had just encountered

Now you would think the owner of this child would be full of remorse at leaving the poor mite to wander so adventurously towards said glass door. Oh no, the female guardian or mother ran to offspring and began to remonstrate with the Baristas for allowing said child to stray as far as the door and protested, "What sort of place is this that don't have stickers on the glass stating this is glass!"

What next I think to myself, Health Warnings outside the shop? 'This establishment serves hot liquids, has hard floors and the volume of conversation may be sensitive to the human ear, possibly not suitable for adults, children and small animals'.

Calm descended as free rounds of coffee and cakes were served up by the Baristas and TLC is administered to the injured darling. Witnessing this display of human kindness, I wondered if there was any chance of getting in on the act, given all the emotional anxiety I had just experienced, a free cappuccino and a slice of lemon drizzle seemed quite appealing.

But no, it was not to be, the crèche rapidly decamped with one bruised child, lots of free drinks and cake plus loyalty cards so full with credit it would be several months before they would need to use their own funds.

Owners and Baristas must now wait for the solicitor's letter for a personal injury claim!

The little darlings!

2. Facial Knotweed

So far this morning I have, unintentionally, overheard a great new idea which, according to the two highly-charged men in the next booth is "mega," their words not mine.

They seem to be pre-occupied in their own twilight zone, completely oblivious to their surroundings and the fact all in the room are privy to their eureka moment, this revolutionary new discovery.

Not suited and booted are these two eager beavers. Jeans and Jumpers are the order of the day with ankle length mustard coloured socks, above which a good four inches of raw white flesh is visible; slightly off-putting. However, to continue, they are each sporting the now popular pointed tan shoes, which in the 60's we used to call winkle pickers. Both are heavily bearded in the Rasputin style and in their early twenties, however, the forest of facial hair makes them look more like forty.

They must be celebrating as more drinks are ordered, not coffee for these fine fellows but green tea, which in hindsight could be the recipe for promoting the Japanese knotweed of a beard which consumes their previously cherub-like features. Not even their own mothers would recognise them now.

Time out as they consume drinks and engage in banal conversation about their weekend activities. I switch off.

It's not too long before they resume business and their noise level increases as they become more animated, hand and arm gestures are used to the extreme as they continue unabated. Plug sockets are required –there under the seats guys! - Laptops are mobilised, and messages sent.

Soon mobile phones ring, glad tidings are exchanged with their 'brose', their words not mine and a meeting is organised. I and all in cafe now know the venue, time and yes, the secret single agenda item.

Apparently, it's tonight, at 7pm Valley Lodge Hotel, name of B. Ollox & Co, not sure their board of directors and shareholders would be too pleased with the 'brose' sharing this info with all and sundry.

So, my dilemma is this, do I either move out of earshot and avoid a migraine or stay and hear more of this idea which they believe is 'future-busting,' again their words.

Pass me the aspirin please.

3. 'Who's Beryl Burton'

The silence was broken by the arrival of the Denton Cycling Club, all fourteen of them, from now on referred to as D.C.C.s. In they marched, dressed from head to toe in green and yellow lycra, the club's colours, a giant centipede.

Men in lycra, what a site to behold, all in step like a brigade of guards, their cycling boots crunching the hard-wooden floor of the coffee shop.

I say men as the body hugging all in one lycra suits leave little to the imagination, exposing every bump, bulge of the occupant, yes, they were obviously of the male species.

Garry - as I later found the team leader was called - was heading the charge for the counter. All Baristas to the pump as various combinations of coffee are ordered from the basic Americano to the exotic frappe' latte Mocha, not as the Barista points out to Garry, to be confused with the frappe latte classic, which take an age to make. Fourteen drinks and pastries in one order, boy would I like the points on that loyalty card.

Now it's at this point that I always feel sympathy for the next customer to arrive immediately after the DCCs, because they haven't a hope in hell of being served their caffeine fix for the next twenty minutes as the Baristas slave away on the large order.

Enter the victim, let's call him Eric. One can see the immediate look of horror followed by disappointment on arriving at the end of this human centipede. All hope of the quick fix has gone. His dilemma, either be patient and feel the pain or look for another shop.

It gets worse, for in burst two more D.C.C.s, it's the tandem pair who have been lagging behind the rest. The first one, obviously female is small of height, thin of face, now to be known as the pilot. She is followed by the male, whom I have christened the engine. He is a barrel of a man whose body will certainly test the structure of his lycra suit and thighs like the pistons from the Titanic.

Garry to Pilot and Engine, "What's your order I'm in the chair?" - more points on the loyalty card. It's at this point one can feel a certain amount of pity for the victim, not only has he been usurped by the late arrival of the two lycras, but they order two frappe latte classic, which we all now know take an age to make.

Peace descends on the room as the now sixteen members settle into their seats and Eric, he of a patient nature and has acquired a BP of 210/120 finally gets his cappuccino.

Pondering the site of this lycra-clad group it occurs to me that except for Engine, they have probably attended a course on colonic irrigation to achieve their snake-like figures. No doubt Garry organised a block booking acquiring masses of loyalty points.

The conversation that drifts my way is technical, on the merits of the new Japanese gears verses the original Italian campagnolia gears, cogs, timings and ratios all of which is the cyclist version of Esperanto. Further discussion reveals that the British cyclist

Reg Harris OBE, the Lancashire lad World and Olympic champion is buried at the local *Church.

"Fascinating, but what about Beryl Burton OBE, multi-world champion?" shouts the pilot. "The best female cyclist ever, could show you boys a thing or to."

No response from the guys and Pilot looks well angered. I can foresee a lively exchange at their next AGM, as Pilot claims sexism and discrimination against female cyclists.

"Well, what about Beryl Burton"? shouts Pilot again.

"Who's Beryl Burton" asked Garry.

"Who's Beryl Burton"? is the echo from Pilot, repeating the sentence again with growing anger.

Now I'm thinking, 'come on Garry even I've heard of this famous lass from Yorkshire. She's won more medals than you've had Frappe's.'

"He's winding you up," shouts Engine. "Don't let him get under your skin." Skin! There's hardly enough of her to cover a bike saddle.

Moving on my interest continues as Garry is describing to the group an altercation and near accident he had with the driver of a 4x4 motor car. They obviously know each other well as Garry knows his occupation, referring to him as a 'real banker'!

Finally, the clatter of marching boots on the floor announces the departure of the D.C.C.s, the human centipede is on its way out. To their immense credit they have left the tables clear of all debris, not a paper cup in site, chairs put away and as clean as when they arrived.

On their way in, however, is the crèche with their fully mechanised army of perambulators plus occupants. I can't imagine those tables remaining that clean for long, or in such tidy manner after use.

I exit the shop and deep in thought, cross the road to my car reflecting on the good manners of the older generation in lycra.

"Hey grandad, watch where you're going you banker," shouts Engine as we have a near miss.

I bet Beryl Burton never used that language.

Note: *I have visited the church during the summer months when each Sunday they hold a garden fête with homemade cakes, tea and coffee. The teas and food are wonderful however, the coffee is an acquired taste!

4. My Bobby Ewing Moment

"Well Frank do you want to tell us your story?"
Who said that? Where did that come from? Oh, it's Carol the facilitator at the group I attend each Wednesday.
"You must go to Rehab they told me, fantastic I thought, never been to the Middle East, then I end up here!"
Kaffine Organisation Stop Addiction or K*OSA* for short.
She's been running these sessions for two years after being asked to leave Illy coffee company following an incident in the shop one day. She was caught mixing the beans and was the worse for wear after a cocktail of Brazilian and Columbian best brew.
It's been four weeks now since I had my referral to attend the group. It's ten am, normally prime time for a caffeine shot, however, part of the deal is you have to attend the self-help group and discuss 'one's condition,' as they call it, more commonly known as addiction. So, we meet at the local scout hut me and ten other haunted soles.

I start my story.......

"My first recollection of coffee goes way back to 1966 and journeys to the Alasia cafe' in Manchester, billed as the cities first Italian café. It was run by two Italians and can be better described in the vernacular of the day as a greasy spoon. Anyhow to a 16-year old frothy coffee was a revelation in those days.

This was a Sunday night out. We always occupied the same table in the window, coffee at nine pence in old money was all you needed for a couple of hours out with your mates in Manchester, there for 6pm and back home for 8:30pm on the 98 bus.

For the next couple of years I had to make do with tea and coffee from the works vending machine, totally indescribable, however, one got used to it after a while.

Later, during my early twenties, I started to experiment more with cold drinks, red wine, white, well any colour would do after the first bottle. Then came Jamaica in 1973 and the rum, followed by gout, then the vitamin B shots, more of which later.

Around 1999 I started work for a company that involved quite a lot of travel to various parts of the UK. This meant early starts which would often find me at my destination, say Newcastle at 9am and in dire need of a caffeine shot. This renewed my relationship with coffee through various local cafes, from 'Tom's Top Breakfasts' in Lincoln to 'Bertie's Tea Rooms' in Harrogate and 'The Bean House' in Wales.

Business Meetings were held in hotels who started to offer drinks through a franchise they had bought from the high street coffee chains. The quality improved and I eventually promoted myself to visiting the Starbucks, Nero and Costa branches irrespective of where I was or the time of day. I tried all types from latté, mocha, frappe and finally settled on the following as my coffee of choice.

"A small cappuccino, slightly dry, no chocolate and served in a takeout cup."

One was usually sufficient, then slowly it crept up to two when the initial shot wasn't having the desired effect. On one occasion I had three all very dry, I should explain the very dry is a double shot with little milk and loads of froth. This usually left me wide eyed and rather scary looking.

Then I started to drink at home, early morning, then off for my corporate fix. Afternoon would see me resorting to instant coffee, sacrilege, however just the smell was enough to keep me going.

Furthermore, my trip to the US, for Ben and Emily's wedding only fed my need for caffeine as I found the delights of 'Fodgers' freshly ground coffee. Everywhere I went in the US people served hot ground coffee and it was good, very good!

It gets worse. On their trips to the US I had my relatives bring back different strains of beans and I bought a percolator. I had involved innocent people in my cravings for the dreaded bean.

I started to have hot sweats and experienced blurred vision. I would be cranky some days and as high as a kite on others. It was then that I was forced to see the doctor and well that leads me here today."

I stopped my 'share,' exhausted, as I had unburdened myself to others who knew how it felt. Some were recovering from the excesses of the bean, others from the tea leaf, hot chocolate and the worst, Bovril.

"Thanks for sharing," said the group leader and then I started to hear people singing. I couldn't make it out at first then it sounded like , ...yes it was, it was Earl Brown from the group Hot Chocolate....Next a woman's voice....."Shall I turn the radio off and would you like a hot drink, now you've decided to wake up?"

Wow, what a night-mare that was.

A hot coffee first thing in the morning was just what I needed. I lay back as Moi arrived with my delicious coffee…

"Here you go," she said. "A nice cup of hot milk, mustn't be late for your meeting this morning its almost nine o'clock"….!!!

Hell………………

5. Business to Business

Even before the door to the shop opened the sound of someone talking very loud precipitated the arrival of John (hereafter known as the voice).

Here we go I thought, and in walked the 'voice', tall, thin, clean shaven head and an enormous Moses beard that draped from his face. With his mobile phone lodged precariously under his chin he approached the Barista who patiently waited for a gap in his conversation before asking for his order.

Light laser-blue suit, no belt and something that always amazed me, tan shoes, completed by a white shirt, no tie of course and the obligatory shoulder bag hanging around his neck.

So, there he was totally consumed in the conversation with Pete.

"No not that one," he berated Pete, "The other one near the garage, you arse!"

It transpired his mate, had gone to the wrong coffee shop and 'voice' was unintentionally pointing out his error, to the entire collection of patrons in the shop.

Seconds later Arse appeared. There stood the mirror image of 'voice', peas in a pod.

My thoughts turned to the poor Barista, still waiting patiently to take their order, not a sigh or a break in her smile, she probably wanted to knock their heads together, however, I am sure that would contravene company policy. Probably resulting in a demotion to trainee Barista and a criminal record for GBH.

Finally, and without even a glance at the Barista came the order, "Two cappuccinos with double shots."

Descending on a table in the middle of the shop they begin to set out their stall. Laptops are produced; cable sockets are sought. Without a care in the world and in great detail they are deep in conversation. An hour goes by during which a further order of drinks of similar potency are ordered.

Their discussion is conducted at such a volume that one cannot help but overhear the detail of what I can only believe to be a highly confidential matter. Apparently, this involves a new pharmaceutical product that the 'voice's company has concocted, and he wants Arse to trial the drug in what he terms a 'customer faced reflection programme.' More generally known as customer feedback.

Their discussion continues for a while longer, both seem totally oblivious to the fact they are conducting this in an open environment amongst, now some very irritated and amused fellow customers. Eventually they stand to leave, no handshakes for these two, it's now the full-on style man hug.

Having unwittingly notified the entire congregation of the shop of this highly secret product and how it will be trialled, a thought crosses my mind. Should I buy shares in this company that I now know so much about? Maybe.......

Post script...I never did buy shares in the company, maybe the drug wasn't all it was cracked up to be, something called Viagra.

6. 'Bridge' in Colour.

Over the next half an hour, the four lively gals of the bridge club arrive. Yes, I know it's not politically correct, however, that's what they are in this story. I have observed them every Tuesday for the past month as they descend on the coffee shop from 11.00 am.

Various drinks are ordered as their number gathers at the centre table in the shop, now occupied by a gregarious gaggle of fifty somethings. Their individual perfumes form an invisible wall around the group combining to deliver a toxic and highly expensive aura, a 'no-go' area for non-members. The head perfumer, a gal with an alarming orange tan, introduces the playing cards and a silence descends on the group. Pairs have already been agreed and sit as per the rules, one pair North South and the other East West, thirteen cards are delivered to each member of the lesser tanned group.

The next few minutes are spent re-arranging their cards which they hold fan like in hands with finger nails well-manicured at the local Korean nail bar and sprinkled with glitter in various colours. From what seemed like a meeting of the local WI, has now taken on a more sinister form.

The previously chatty four are now in mental combat with their oppos. Hand signals are made, and mutterings can be heard between each pair as they agree strategies.

There is no financial gain to winning, no money is involved. However, that doesn't make it less serious, pride and ego are at stake here. Occasionally the silence is broken with mention of auction, bid and contract, followed by further deathly periods of quiet as presumably they consider their options. Out of the blue the orange one declares, "Grand slam thirteen of thirteen, that's 1500 vulnerable points."

Well I ask you what the hell does that mean!?

The orange glow has now given way to a bright red facial flush, the pressure is on, either that or the menopause is about to begin. I hear reference to, "three no trumps, two no trumps," my god surely one Donald is enough. An hour later and game over, the scores are revealed, head perfumer dissolves into a lighter shade of orange as it is revealed she and her partner have lost the last few rubbers.

Viewing the rules of Bridge, I find there are a number of versions such as Rubber, Contract and Duplicate Bridge. The rules seem to have their origins in 1886 when a Mr John Collinson first introduced them. The term Bridge is derived from the Russian game of 'Whist' known as Biritch, also the name of a local town in that area of the world. Furthermore, it appears to have been popular in the USA during the 1930's through a certain Mr. Ely Culbertson of Chicago.

It, (Bridge) also has International Olympic Committee (IOC) status as one of only two mind sports recognised by the IOC, the other being Chess.

Well that's another Tuesday over with, the dark brown wooden chair legs scrape the mosaic tiled floor announcing the departure of half the group. The usual air kisses are exchanged as the losers depart.

The winning pair stay on for a victory coffee and spend an animated half-hour conducting a character assassination of the losers.

Can't wait for next week.

7. Ace Reporter in A&E

Date of reporting 7th December

I have spent more time than I care to remember in the local hospital over the last few weeks.

Waiting-rooms in particular, have a profound effect on my physical and mental wellbeing. It is as though the anaesthetic is seeping through the operating-theatre walls and I rapidly give way to slumber. Slowly descending into sleep, it's a full-on totally catatonic unconscious state of mind, the kind one probably enjoyed as a one-year-old.

Considering my usual sleep pattern is erratic, does this mean I have to spend every night in my local A&E to achieve my recommended eight hours?

Today is no exception. Sitting in the MRI waiting room, I decide on a coffee in the sure knowledge a shot of caffeine will delay the onset of slumber. So, it's off to the (RVS) Royal Voluntary Service cafeteria. Now there's a throwback to the 1950's. Staffed by ladies of a certain maturity, smiles meet me as I order a cappuccino,

"Sorry my lovey, we only do instant," is the reply from Doris.

Her name badge is all the information I need to reply, "yes fine Doris anything with caffeine and a chocolate biscuit please"

She finds this hilarious and shouts the order to the lady with kettle and large bottle of instant Nescafé. The orchestra of noise in the room is drowned by Doris's booming voice of authority.

I find a table and open my newspaper, excellent now for the caffeine.

Not so, a cup of hot chocolate arrives. The detail of my order has been lost in translation between Doris and the head barrister, namely Rosie, as per her name badge.

Again, more hilarity as Doris informs all who will listen about this minor incident, which, had it occurred in one of the national coffee chains would probably result in a P45 for the barrister or retraining on inter-personal skills.

Spread newspaper on table and take in the news reports from my favourite right wing press. Once again my choice of reading is much to the displeasure of son and heir Ben, who believes I should take a more informed publication without political bias. If you can find such a literary treasure, please let me know.

Back to the paper, I am taking in the resent reports from the rumour factory of possible transfers in the football market when I realise I have read the same paragraph three times!

The words are just not sinking in, "concentrate" I think to myself, same thing happens, can't remember a word. Looking up I hear, along with everyone else in the Cafe', the telephone conversation the young nurse is conducting on her mobile, so that's what is interfering with my wiring.

After several more minutes of this intrusion, there's only one thing to do, terminate reading of right wing press and listen intently to her now very interesting chat. Why not, she is talking loud enough to wake everyone in wards 1 to 7 and the dead?

I adjust my seating to a more lateral position to ensure I hear more clearly and a better view of the ear basher.

"Have you told them that's it and make sure you pack the black bag it has all the necessary clothing"? Are her instructions.

Adding "best if you leave that until the last minute you never know which one he will want you to ware."

This is now real time drama and far more interesting than the daily blurb, paper discarded to the bin. This is great material and I quickly reach for pen and paper, there's a story in a story here. Suddenly I am transformed into the ace reporter from FOX NEWS, why fake a story when there's one unfolding in front of me.

"this is the last time, it's doing my back in" she reveals.

Wow this is promising, a possible scoop here, maybe a National Award, Journalist of the Year. I must rein myself in, calm down.

Where is this going, how long can I sit and take notes without her noticing? Must stop, this is bordering on voyeurism, and just as I decide to quit she finishes her call with,

"Just make sure he knows, it's so embarrassing with all those people watching "!

Dilemma, do I follow her and ask for an exclusive, or stay and retrieve my paper from the bin? No contest, I'm off my chair, ace reporter on the move, following nursie down past A&E, beyond the chapel of rest, which always left me feeling a bit weird when passing those doors, left at the rancid coffee machine, then on via the vampire unit, commonly known as the blood test area.

I'm now in the main corridor weaving in and out of patients in wheel chairs, on crutches and porters pushing empty trollies. At this speed I'm an accident waiting to happen and so it nearly does with a pregnant lady, who judging by her size looks as though she could have four on board. Due to the weight of her precious cargo, she is unable to take any avoiding action. Consequently, it is up to me to do an emergency stop, thereby avoiding an earlier than planned entry into this world of her four passengers.

I am sufficiently chastised by 'she who is about to increase the population' and the accompanying porter. Somewhat sheepish I give my apologies and then as I am about to continue the chase, I see the staff noticeboard on the corridor wall. Scatter dust in gold and silver has been used to create stars which surround the statement printed in bright blue:

12.30pm to 1.30pm 7th December 2017
In the main theatre (provided not in use)

Rehearsals for the Christmas pantomime vacancies for two people front and back end of the donkey'. No experience necessary.

Certainly made an ass of me!

8. The New-Man Dad

Here he comes, the new man dad.

He steers the buggy containing the oldest offspring towards the door, boom! It's automatic and allows him entry.

The latest addition to the clan, a six-month old pink cherub is strapped firmly to his chest. Poor mite spends most of the journey looking skywards at this strange being, his father, who has the fashionable Rasputin style beard, his face partially lost in this black mop. What a way to start life, in a huge follicle growth. He'll be seeing a shrink in later years.

Now there are three levels in this coffee shop, each one with three steps, not easy at the best of times when navigating two large lattes to a table. So, instead of taking a seat on the ground floor our new Dad decides to manoeuvre his way up three floors with family in tow. Decamping he parks pram containing junior, I say pram these things are more like tractors, then he off-loads supplies. Wow, it's like Boots chemists, a bottle or cream for everything.

It isn't too long before first-born decides to make his presence felt. So as new dad tries to pacify number one son, his worst fears are realised. Junior, not to be left out joins in and we have a symphony of wailing the like of which drives everyone, over a certain age out of the shop. Mutterings of "kids," "can't even go for a quiet cup of coffee these days," and the inevitable tutting is offered.

On other days I have seen the same people bringing in their own grandchildren and talking the language of goo-goo. The elders doth protest too much, me thinks!
(with apologies to the bard.)

New dad needs help and mum's nowhere to be seen. His university degree in Agriculture hasn't prepared him for this. Try as he might nothing seems to quell the rebellion, now with wailing in stereo. Finally, the cavalry arrives, its mum and, boy is he, never mind the kids, pleased to see her!

We all know what they want and, oh no! modesty takes a back seat, outcome the refuelling tanks to satisfy their hunger.

Voices can be heard registering their discomfort with the, "Not in a public area," to the cheeky, "Which one's the double espresso?"

Decamping, the family decide to leave, half empty cups and plates adorn their table, the remainder of junior's mini capo' and cake cover the floor.

Why would you feed a child of that age caffeine and a sugar bomb? I bet that doesn't appear in the NHS good parenting guide.

Exiting the door, Dad pushes tractor with junior to the edge of the pavement ready to cross the road. Junior is probably having the fright of his life at this point. At his eye level these fast-moving coloured pieces of metal are racing past him, what is he to make of this? Is Father Rasputin offering him up as a sacrifice to these beasts?

Mum steps in and takes control turning the tractor sideways on to the pavement and junior is safe. Now all he can see are the cyclists parking their bikes outside the café, and at that level of sight he has full view of the lycra clad male anatomy, he will probably be scarred for life.

Mum to the rescue.

9. Darth Vader

Authors note: Any reference to people, dogs or cats living or dead is purely coincidental. With the exception of the author, no humans, dogs or cats were hurt in the writing of this story.
....

Darth Vader (DV) walked in through the open door, well when I say the prince of darkness it was actually the man from the security company.

Dressed in all black, shin pads and elbow pads in place and the necessary helmet with visor and protective neck shield he at least looked the part.

It was Monday 11:40 am and like clockwork, he appeared, strolling in with suitcase in hand to collect the takings from sales of the magic bean, the giver of mental highs. Why always the same time and day of the week, have they not seen the movies where the bad guys always case the joint?

He gives the usual nod of acknowledgement to the Baristas and strolls through to the office at the rear of the shop. How do they know he's Kosher, with his visa down he could be masquerading as a guard only to get to the safe? Well he's in, all five foot two inches of him, blow hard enough and he would fall over.

And another thing why doesn't he arrive at the rear of the building instead of putting us, the paying customers at risk of a frontal attack from would be chancers?

Ten minutes pass and he emerges with the case chained to his wrist - a Stanley knife would result in a quick release - that by now is presumably full of the dosh. He stops at the counter and collects his cappuccino in takeout cup. Now, I ask you what use is a security man carrying a suitcase full of money in one hand and a coffee cup in the other? What's more the door is closed, and he needs help from a customer to let him out.

Outside he puts down the coffee cup on the pavement and with the free hand releases the chain and places the case through what looked like a cat flap in the rear of the van. Which by the way has been parked outside for the whole time on double yellows and blocking traffic in both directions.

He returns to the front passengers' side and the van drives off, so I assume there is also a second person the driver.

I muse over the events of the past half hour and think how easy it might be to relieve the monotony of his day and unburden him with the responsibility of that cash. A little more reconnaissance on my part and I am sure I could come up with a plan. Why not, since being forced to graze in this meadow of retirement I need something to exercise my imagination and this might just be the answer, plus I need a long expensive holiday, preferably though not in Strangeways.

Over the next few weeks I continue to observe and make notes.

And so it was that five weeks later on the first Monday of the month I had my plan, two willing accomplices whom I christened R2 and D2, my code name is Boss, two lively fox terriers from the local kennels, plastic Aldi bags, camera and our getaway tickets to Crewe.

At 11.20 am the shop is occupied by the usual crowd of would be entrepreneurs and importantly dog walkers. R2 was positioned on the ground floor with the two terriers. D2 and I were on the top floor nearest the office door casually sipping our coffee. In walked Dark Vader, nods to the Baristas and walks up the stairs to the back office passing me and D2 on the way. As soon as he disappeared through the door I gave the signal to R2 who let the terriers off their leads and gave them a bone each. Have you ever seen dogs fighting over a bone? Well here we had a pack every dog in the place wanted a piece of, the chewy marrow and our boys were having none of it. Newspapers flew, coffee cups crashed and owners either stood in horror or waded in to restrain their canine friends.

At precisely that moment D2 and I followed the guard into the back office and caught him unawares just as the safe was opened. He looked shocked, surprised and with the two of us standing their menacingly, I gave him my instructions which were crystal clear, "Strip to your underpants now!" Why I had decided to employ the tactic of humiliation I am not sure, probably watching too many episodes of 'Homeland.' However, it worked.

As D2 filled the Aldi plastic bags with the bean money he dutifully obliged and standing there in all his glory, I took several pictures which I felt sure he would never want to see the light of day, hence I felt our anonymity was secured. His Dark Vader suit was bagged and all that was left to do was mask his mouth, piercing a hole for him to breath and secure his hands and ankles with tape.

We then exited via the fire door at the back, dropped his clothes in the big green refuge bin and walked casually to the railway station where we were to meet R2. In the shop however, there was an uproar with accusations flying around of who started what, calls for the police to separate the dog owners and the RCPCA to administer TLC to the canine protagonists, whilst we met R2 and boarded the train for Crewe.

....

Well, that's how it should have happened, unfortunately there were one or two unforeseen problems along the way. Firstly, my two fellow accomplices backed out and so there were no terriers, hence no distraction. None the less I decided to go it alone, convinced I could pull this off. To replace the terriers, I borrowed the neighbour's cat and carried this inside a large satchel, unfortunately the poor creature was claustrophobic and was having the longest panic attack in cat history.

I took up a position on the ground floor and waited for DV. On arrival I hesitated until he was up the stairs and out of sight, then let the cat out of the bag, no pun intended. In fact, that part of the event went better than the original plan as Kitty ran amok, spitting and clawing at any canine that dared to approach, she was a huge success.

This cat fight was my cue to disappear and so I walked up the stairs into the office and there was DV about to open the safe. I pulled out my camera, why? What was I hoping to do with that? Anyhow that was the last thing I remembered until I came to on the floor. Seems Mr five foot two inches is a black belt in karate, taekwondo, judo, he's the man. Chief trainer at the security company.

Later in the A&E department at Manchester Royal Infirmary I was interviewed by the police who charged me with no more than disturbing the peace and aiming a camera at a security guard. The only picture it captured was of the office ceiling as I lay flat out.

The coffee chain, however, took a different view that really hurt. For my adventure I have been black-listed from every coffee shop in a twenty-mile radius of Manchester.

With my arm in plaster and a neck brace my activities from home have been limited. Occasionally I have taken a short stroll passing my neighbour's house where kitty, she of the aggressive nature, sits quite content on the bonnet of her owners' car.

Apparently, it had taken three RSPCA officers two hours to coax kitty from behind the bar, by which time she was hungover following a mixture of skimmed, semi and full fat milk.

She views me through her emerald green slanted eyes, appears to smile and lick her lips as though saying, "Hey Boss, when's the next gig?"

I lapse into a catatonic state.

10. A Full House

Why not come with me this morning and I'll give you an insight in 'real time' of what's going on in what I call the office, the coffee shop.

Check the time? It's 11.30 am. Mind the step, there's a slate missing, and I am sure that will be a classic Personal Injury Claim sometime soon. The injured party, however, will probably have to wait years for compensation, eventually receiving payment in loyalty points!

That's it, automatic door, long gone are the signs 'push', 'open', all done by sensors now, find a seat and I'll get the drinks in.

Can you see the look of anger on the faces of those at the front of the queue when the latest arrivals grab the most comfortable chairs before ordering drinks! If looks could kill, passive aggression is in abundance today.

"What will you have?"

"A Mocha, ok?"

Yes, those armchairs will do nicely, the paper is on the rack, no not the Times, the other one with big letters. That's it the daily right-wing propaganda.

"It's all the same," you say?

Well I wouldn't mention that to Ben and Emily if I were you, I've had many an ear-bashing on that subject, in stereo.

Here you go, one mocha in a takeout cup. It won't be too long now before one has to pay a premium for using disposable cups, which will eventually become a collector's item. (see chapter Antique Road Show)

Yes, in answer to your question, they do let dogs in accompanied by owners, although sometimes I feel it is the other way around. Dogs usually behave better.

"Yes, I did see that."

"I know, I feel the same."

Ordering a drink from the barista whilst on their phone. There's another, just as we discussed, phone is ringing and owner answers in the face of barista. Now everyone must wait until their call is over.

Refuse to serve them until they put phone away, that's a great idea, although someone will claim phone-ism, discrimination and sue the company.

"Please hold, your call is important to us, " now the answer machine is in on the act.

You can tell when it starts to get too busy for the baristas. Aurora, the manager, goes quiet and in to overdrive, multitasking, making several versions of coffee from the bean and microwaves the new offering of instant porridge.

Oops! here she goes and let's fly with a shot of her native Italian, sounds like she is cursing the microwave, however she smiles and mutters something about wanting a holiday. Who can blame her, after a day serving numerous Cheshire caffeine junkies, she deserves one.

Caramel this and fudge that, with extra shot, and a marshmallow do-dar, you'd have to be a Dyson-robot not to be affected by this bunch of caffeine connoisseurs.

"Well, will you look at that?" See, as I mentioned to you previously. You have the dogs shaking off their flees, bikers in lycra, the bridge gals covered in orange tan and the Rasputin bearded business guys all in together today. Oh, and not forgetting the little darlings with their baby cappos, parents and grandad.

It's a full house!

11. The next world leader

It's pouring 'cats and dogs' and I am miles from my favourite caffeine rest home. So, needs must, and I descend on a local, what shall we call it, bakers with a 1980's coffee machine. Wet and somewhat disorientated I order a standard coffee and well that's new, "Find a seat dear and I'll bring it over," calls Deirdre the assistant. Name tag is a giveaway and I always use them.

It arrives, its hot, looks like coffee, smells nearly like coffee and you know what they say if that's the case then it must be coffee. Unfortunately, that's where the similarity ends because it didn't taste like any coffee I have ever experienced. Served up in a large souvenir cracked mug with the logo, 'Come to Morecambe for your sunny summer holidays'. There's an oxymoron if ever I have heard one; Morecambe and sunny in the same sentence!

It could have been worse, might have been a mug, and there are many, from Stretford Rangers. Sorry boys however, you know the game by now, we each take a cheap shot whenever we can. The only thing I will say in your defence is that in the 1990's you had a team mostly made up of boys from Manchester, that's good, oh and some kid from East London who kicked us out of the world cup. Remember Sermeoni?

It's cold. However, I'm now starting to feel the warming benefit of this coffee-like substance when in walk the younger generation. Puffer jackets, shoulder bags and trainers are the dress code with talk of going to Uni.

The three sixteen-year olds, all potential future leaders of the 'free world' amble in through the open door. One female and two males, possible transgenders, who knows what's politically correct anymore? I'm bound to offend someone.

My vote is on the female as next world leader. Thoughtful, a praying mantis, poor boys full of bravado, they haven't a chance and look mesmerised in her presence.

So, what is the preferred diet of this generation? Chia loaf, bird seed bake, goats milk biscuits, stuffed snake head with quinoa? Not so, snacks are purchased which are all high in sugar, fat and the obligatory salt, designed to guarantee an extended tour in A&E at some future date. Let's hope they have the sense to acquire private health insurance or an employer who provides such cover. Note. Beware of pre-existing conditions and the small print.

Their choice of clothing interests me. The boys have not yet progressed to the laser-blue suits with tan shoes, hopefully fashions will have changed before they get to that point. They wear carrot-top jeans, hanging precariously above their rear. You know the type, similar to those worn by the inmates at the state penitentiary, belts removed in case they decide to do themselves an injury.

Trainers, without the laces tied, why? I answer my own question instantly, because it's the fashion. I had my time with those classic combat jackets from the Army and Navy store in Piccadilly, 10/-shillings or 50p in new money. To finish this ensemble, they are wearing conventional white-collar shirts outside their trousers no tie, very trendy.

The girl by contrast is in full uniform with school badge, dark navy jacket and top, skirt well not sure about that, looks like a wide belt, and black Doc Martin shoes. The tights however whilst the standard dark colour are ripped, east to west at the knee on both legs, displaying bear anaemic-looking skin. Does she know I wonder, has anyone dared to tell her? Forget it, it's the fashion.

Hey, here's a new fashion idea which they may be interested in, why not start to wear clothes inside out? Jeans, jackets – wouldn't work with shoes though – the linings of clothes are often more colourful and interesting than the exterior?

They speak in a different language, a shorthand version of something that used to be called The Queens English, abbreviations for nearly every word and all whilst simultaneously on their iPhones. To give you some idea their vocabulary contains reference to 'fintech world of change and how millennials are reshaping banking'. 'Venmo, Klarna' and 'Bit Coins', don't ask, google it and you tell me!

I would convey more of the conversation to you, however, apart from the occasional word, its way beyond my understanding. She, talks at length of cryogenics, that's one word I recognise and then mentions age limitation. That starts to send alarm bells ringing as those two words used in the same sentence are disturbing for someone who knows what happened to Walt Disney. Throughout, the others, whilst still texting 'keep in touch,' with the occasional 'ugh' and then she, the new world leader in waiting, starts on again abut cryogenics and suggests the words, 'age termination' instead of 'limitation.'

Alarming….? Very!

So, there you have it three for the future with a combined age of forty-eight. In ten years will they occupy positions as head of google, a parliamentarian, euro minister (we may yet have another vote) will any of these so-called jobs even exist in their future? Well let's hope there are millions of sixteen-year olds like them all over this small planet of ours, thinking of making this a better place. Although, the least said about cryogenics the better.

Time is up, and they are off to do homework, well maybe that's a thing of the past. Plan the revolution? Been done before! Next cyber-attack? Nothing new there either. Here's a bit of advice from the old guard.

Just go home and enjoy being sixteen.

12. Jeff and the Geordies.

It never ceases to amaze me how uninhibited people are when discussing their most private and personal affairs in the open arena of a coffee shop.

They are either, nose to nose across a table with their latest confidant or laid back in one of the arm chairs, holding court and gesticulating their more interesting points with a wave of their hand in a Queen-like manner. To be clear, the latter is usually performed by the male of the species.

The recipients of this ear bashing are transfixed with the colourful detail and join in, topics range from the three D's, divorce, death or duties to a recent court case or business deals that are mega! The former is usually a conversation between the platinum blonde - I kid you not - and her clones. In the case I am destined to hear all in her presence seem to have a view on how she should, "Skin Jeffery for as much as you can pet."

"Way I," said clone number two, "You canna let him get awaa with that pet."

I mean, I don't want to know, and I am sure Jeffery wouldn't be too pleased to hear I am privy to his leasing arrangements for his Bentley and Porsche. Blondie happily tells all it's a tax scam through his IT firm, which, at the moment, is experiencing a capital crisis. Aren't we all dear!

Well, that's the story Jeffrey has told Blondie, his business is not in a good place. However, her legal eagle whom she plans to see later today has investigated and unearthed more information that casts doubt on his version.

Seems Jeff (I feel I know him well enough now to use the abbreviated version) hasn't been quite as transparent about his assets as is required in these circumstances. They, the clones each have a tale to tell about 'a friend' - "a right bonnie lass" - in a similar situation, does this make blondie feel better? I think not. But the clones are now on a roll with stuff which I am sure boarders on slander. All I can gather is that Jeff, who I now feel a certain amount of sympathy with is – metaphorically speaking - in for a right kicking.

Enough is enough, so I gather my bits and pieces, paper, coffee, coat etc. and decamp to a less comfortable seat yet thankfully way out of earshot from the Macbeth like coven of witches. ("Dubble, dubble, toil and trouble," were never more apt). I really don't want to hear any more just leave me to concentrate on the sports page and obituaries column of the Times. That's another thing, whenever I read the shop's copy of the Times, the obituaries page is always 'dog eared' as though all previous readers have made straight for the 'who's no longer with us page.'

"I tell you Josh, we gonna have to move on this and do some serious recruitment for the stats to fly."

Who's that? Where did that come from? And what the hell does it mean? Serious recruiting - is there any other sort - stats to fly and where does the word 'gonna' appear in the Concise Oxford English Dictionary? Gonorrhoea that's a word however, I don't think that's what they mean.

All these questions are suddenly upon me as I am forced to take in this new language from the group seated at the centre table.

This is a far cry from when I held meetings with business colleagues, usually in the reception areas of hotels. We would always head for a corner spot, face the room and pull chairs in close. Mafia like in appearance, however, the last thing we wanted was to be overheard. The waiter arrived with drinks and all conversation stopped, once he was out of earshot we continued. Paranoid, maybe a little however, you never know who's on the next table.

Back to those table dwellers using Esperanto, could I really be bothered moving again? Well as luck would have it they call their meeting to a close, 'praise the Lord'. Engaging in the obligatory man hugs and air kisses, the long goodbye begins and then fizzles out with a few, "ciao mate, ciao darlings," and they are off.

In fact, the place is now empty, peace and silence descend. So, where is this monologue of 'rates of pay and hours worked' coming from? The Baristas obviously unaware of my presence are in open conversation then suddenly the language changes and they are back to their native Polish. Excellent, should they decide to go on strike, I cannot be called as a witness in whatever was to be discussed.

I reflect on how polite these Baristas from the EU and other countries are. They work all hours, don't complain, are extremely patient and make these visits for a caffeine shot, a better place. They deserve a pay rise or at least free refreshments on their fifteen-minute break and a loyalty card.

"Still writing the book"?

At last it's a voice I recognise and a friendly face. It's Steve an ex-colleague with whom I used to work in the 1980's at what was once Samuel Rains and Sons, premier estate agents of Cheshire. Steve and his wife Anita have reviewed one of my previous episodes and made a couple of welcome suggestions on how I might take this collection of odd stories further. We talk for a while and then guess what, I become aware of my own loud voice, luckily there's no one to overhear and write a story!

So, with Steve now well into his Times newspaper and first coffee I reflect on how quick we are, as a species, to judge others and what a hypocrite I might be.

13.Territorial Rights

The trend now is to mark your territory immediately on arrival in the shop even if you are last in the queue at the counter.

I mentioned this in a previous episode and how annoyed those are waiting to be served, who have yet to find a seat. It is somewhat ironic considering they have done the very same thing when they arrive to find themselves at the end of a caffeine queue.

It's akin to the habit, of our German friends, now adopted worldwide of placing towels on hotel sun loungers at four o'clock in the morning, then heading off back to bed, rising again at mid-day.

The latest episode is about to unfold in front of me as a young woman with a dog so small - its mouse-like in appearance - enters and heads straight for the most comfortable and sought-after chair in the place, the chesterfield sofa. Throwing her pink bobble hat onto the seat and tethering 'micky mouse' to the leg of the sofa she heads off to join the queue in the safe knowledge that she has marked her territory.

So, be warned all those patrons present and new arrivals this is her seat. There it lies one lonely item of wool, 'pinkie' which by its very presence states, 'Do not sit here, this is my owner's' seat of choice and she will return.'

You know what happens next.

Yes, correct, the obvious, a man arrives (let's call him Angus) with laptop and seeing the phone socket near to the unoccupied sofa, he descends on the chesterfield as his place of residence for the foreseeable future. Angus disregards pinkie, just manages to avoid treading on 'Micky' thereby turning him into Pâté and begins setting up his office on the facing table.

'Micky' now feeling threatened starts to bark, well it's more like a squeak and owner returns with latté for her, water bowl for Micky and nothing for pinkie. This should be good viewing and it is.

"Excuse me, yes you, I'm sitting here."

"That's OK lassie, I don't mind. I'm sure the sofa is big enough for both of us," replies Angus.

And it was, a large three-seater.

Classic, get out of that lady.

She does, releasing Micky and juggling coffee and water bowl she moves to another table far away from Angus. He, on the other hand, seems unimpressed by events and just wants to get down to work, he, his lap top and the 'forgotten one', still there, alone again, on the sofa is **pinkie!**

14. Geronimo

Sub title: Four Indians and no tepee to go home to.

Today, I decide to view that which is happening outside the coffee shop instead of my introspective view of events within these warm aromatic walls. So, I position myself at a window seat and view the row of shops across the road. A road that is normally parked nose to tail with many types of high end 4x4's and hasn't seen a Vauxhall or Ford for years in this part of leafy Berkshire.

I say normally because on a Monday and Friday it's delivery day for the many restaurants and other eateries that occupy most of the premises along this stretch of London Road. Long gone are the local grocers, off licence and other family businesses. Its estate agents, fashion boutiques and half a dozen charity outlets that now pay the high commercial rates in what was once, a village and now an outpost for half of the Premiership football fraternity in the South.

White delivery vans have congregated to off-load fresh supplies to the restaurants, no sooner has one vacated the parking space than another takes its place. No evidence of supporting the local community here, supplies are from out of town and by the time the chefs have created a delicacy of 'squid a l'orange' cooked in 'Meerkats' milk', sold at an enormous profit, to the gullible patrons. Would they be so eager had they witnessed the kitchen staff engaging in some serious smoking – real ciggies - on their break then wiping their hands on what look, anything but clean, aprons.

I know everyone's allowed a break, "All hail the EU working directive," but seriously in the food industry surely hygiene is a priority and why outside in front of house? If one must use the weed then try the rear of the place, less conspicuous. One hopes they make use of soap and hot water, that's what my aunty Pat drilled into me, 'wash your hands before and after meals.' Although she never said anything about smoking.

A bright blue sky sits aloft, however its deceptive, once outside it is cold, brass-monkey weather. This does not stop four hardy coffee addicts, aged early fifties I guess, from taking up residence at one of the tables outside the shop for their morning fix. They are often here, wrapped in Burberry or Crombie best overcoats, natty scarves and all with masses of silver wire-wool hair. Huddled together at a table, they are in an animated conversation, the subject of which I know not. A heavy-duty glass panel providing a degree of sound proofing. I'll check what's going on, bear with me for a few paragraphs.

By the way, notwithstanding the recent road bypass that has been completed, there is still a reasonable amount of motor traffic that passes through the village. Consequently, CO_2 emissions remain high, particularly as the drivers leave their diesel engines running whilst on delivery.

So, our four fine friends might be outside in the fresh air, however, they are already in a toxic environment when they all decide to light up their e-cigarettes at once. Nothing wrong with that either, each to his own.

I decide to join them outside but at a safe distance as the combined effect of their indulgence is a huge red cloud that sits over their table releasing, not an unpleasant aroma of raspberry and strawberries.

As the minutes go by clouds ascend into the heavens, dilute and fade, then new ones take their place. Smoke signals, that's what it reminds me of. Are these guys sending a message to their families in the northern territories of Watford? What a ridiculous thought.

Then a phone rings, the tone is from Rocky 1 the movie. One of our friends, Lincoln, answers, and so it begins……………

"Sorry babe, I was going to call you, however we had a slight incident last night and had to stay over at George's place."

He's obviously getting an ear full of grief from the caller. However, he continues, "Well it's like this, me and the lads were having a quick drink last night when Geronimo, who had a few too many, takes a swing at George, you know how those two can kick off. Geronimo gets hacked off with Custer always pruning his blonde hair and beard, threatening him with a scalp shave. I manage to quieten things down for a while and we have a few more 'fire waters' then the whole thing started again, it was a massacre. Anyhow me and Horse, you know the crazy one eventually corral them into a taxi and take them back to Custer's little place at 1876 Bighorn Crescent."

"Pocahontas my pet, would I lie to you, that's exactly how it happened, …hello, hello."

"Spoilt child," he thought, she must have hung up as he stares at the iPhone in disbelief.

"Well bugger me," exclaimed Lincoln.

"Not likely," quipped Bill, sitting in his chair and laughing quietly to himself, at what he thought was a highly amusing comment.

Can't say I have any sympathy there, stayed out all night and doesn't even call, no wonder Pocahontas has reservations about the authenticity of this story.

It seems the phone call has instigated a renewal of hostilities between the previously hungover quartet. Voices are raised, there's no peace-pipe here, puffing on their e-ciggies quickens, red and orange clouds form and I decide that there is enough of a smoke screen for me to make a retreat.

Unlike Custer who is probably on his Last Stand.

15. Jennifer the Assassin

I thought I had seen it all, however, the latest visit to my favourite watering hole proved me wrong.

"Now Jennifer, be careful of that man," were the words that registered just milliseconds before feeling the impact. Wheeling around and grimacing with pain I met eye to eye with little Jennifer, the assassin. Her two-wheel bicycle had just rammed my right ankle directly on the spot where I had an achilles-tendon injury some years ago.

"Ouch! you little tinker there are other people in here besides you. Anyway, that bike belongs outside, and as for you, yes you madam, the mother of this child, you should take more responsibility, otherwise she will turn into a right obnoxious delinquent."

That is what I wanted to say. Instead like a weak lamb I smiled and said, "It's OK."

Well, it wasn't, OK.

By now the pain had set in and I was still two customers behind the front of the queue. Relief finally arrived when I received my Cappo, slightly dry of course and then I fell into one of the arm chairs with the assassin far away in the downstairs section of the café. Respite, however, was short- lived as she cycled towards me but stopped at the three steps guarding me from further punishment. Surely, she wouldn't lift the bike up those steps to my floor? She was probably no more than four years old and if she did manage the climb I was sure she wouldn't see five! The steps were like the Great Wall of China to her, a barrier she was unable to navigate. None the less, this little assassin took great delight in staring straight at me for a minute or so. God knows what evil thoughts she was conjuring up, with me in mind as the recipient.

"Come along Jennifer and finish your baby mocha before it goes cold," were the instructions that pierced the air from the mother of assassin.

Yes, off you go, I thought before an injured evil dragon accidentally tips a mug of hot coffee over your bike. I quickly replayed that thought and an image comes to mind of me being hauled off by the police for causing injury to young Jennifer and bike. One quick snap on an iPhone and I would be all over social media, it might go viral, the NSPCC involved.

Hugh Edwards would be reporting the incident on news at ten. I would become a social pariah, the most hated man in Cheshire.

It might seem as though I was hell bent on revenge, however, that was not the case. I had descended into a relaxed mood, catching up on the latest sports news and the, "Who's no longer with us," column of the Times.

Jennifer on the other hand finished her mocha and was back on my case. She rode the bike along the ground floor past all the waiting addicts at the counter where several phone calls were in progress. The coffee machine hissed obediently, and dogs lounged on the floor or sniffed one another which was enough to put me off that Pain-au-Chocolat I had been looking forward to.

She, the assassin, arrived at my barrier. Oh no, she started to climb the steps without the bike and waddled over to my table then uttered the word!

"Sorry"

"It's OK," I said, and this time it was.

16. Journey of a Life Time

(BEAN there done that)

Preamble

Columbia is the third largest producer of the cherry coffee bean in the world. Regional climate change associated with global warming has caused Colombian coffee production to decline since 2006 from 12 million 132-pound bags, the standard measure, to 9 million bags in 2010. The present average is 11.5m bags exported to specific parts of the world.In 2011 UNESCO designated the Coffee Culture Landscape of Columbia a world heritage site.

My name is Arabica and I am known as the king of coffee beans. I live in the shade on the northern reaches of the Andes at a high elevation, which are the best conditions to begin life. My popularity is partly attributed to a Jesuit priest, José Gumilla. In his book The Orinoco Illustrated (1730), he registered the presence of coffee in the mission of Saint Teresa of Tabajé, near where the Meta river empties into the Orinoco. Since then, many generations of my family have travelled to the USA, France and Italy to further their careers.

Today I languish in the shade along with several others on this vine, some red others green in colour and we are the cherries that house the magic bean until ready for picking.

Four years have passed since our plantation and we are now ready for our long-awaited journey. *"OK guys, rest time over, here comes Miguel with his knife,"* looks like we are about to be harvested, but only the ripe red ones. The greens are immature and told to stop being juvenile and grow up.

A quick snip and we join the rest of the family in the cart.

Next is what has been called the 'Ferguson' treatment, the hair dryer or drying process. Then we are tested for taste four times which leaves the 'Marenio' process where we are toasted. We perspire a lot at this point which allows the aroma to develop, its good training.

Having now lost our cherry overcoat we are transferred to a cooler, then vacuum packed and boy is it dark in here. No matter, we are off on our journey from Columbia to where others have 'bean' before.

From the accents I can hear we must be in Italy. Here we undergo another roasting. Then by air, rail and finally road to a well-known high street chain of coffee shops in leafy Cheshire. By now I and my 400 or so compatriots are well tired and nestle down, resting on the top shelf behind the counter in the shop.

During the journey we were jostled around, and I now have a window seat in the transparent side of the packet. From here I witness baristas working feverishly brewing everything from the classic espresso to the outrageous Frappe 'Crème, Salted Caramel & Pistachio, such a show off.

From 7am pastries of Croissant, pana-raison and chocolat Danish, all freshly baked are quickly purchased by the early brigade who need a quick fix before heading off to the motorway.

For payment, most people use something called an app, however, occasionally a loyalty card is produced and bingo there's a free one, although one must purchase nine at £2.60p each to be eligible for this free coffee. So, that's £2.60p times nine equals £23.40p, free? I don't think so.

I can see all this from my vantage point, including the customers and what a mixed bunch they are. Men and women in tight clothing with bicycles, men in suits with jackets that are too small, dogs barking, well they look as though they are, my package is sound proofed.

Also, what should I make of these baskets on wheels that I assume contain the next generation of caffeine addicts. All in a rush to get their daily dose of me, the bean.

Two doggers - dog walking! -have just arrived and it's a couple of grandee mugs that the Barista fills with, hold on, I recognise that bean, it's my cousin Barry, and in he goes. What next, milk that's good then, oh no Fudge cordial followed by thick cream and to add insult to injury chocolate is sprinkled on top! We all had such hopes for Barry on the vine, we thought he was destined to become a latté at the very least.

The manager Olive, reaches for the next packet and she's dropped it on the floor, that's a waste now they will have to sweep up what's left of my uncle Brian. He always was the dark bean of the family, now he's heading for the bin. We are next, scissors slice off the top of the packet and fresh air rushes in as our aroma goes in the opposite direction.

Hello, what's that machine she is working, haven't seen one of those before, but I have heard tales of the dreaded grinder. Oops, too late, in we all go. Its dark and with the blades doing their worst, very noisy.

The result is that I have been cloned thousands of times, all little mess, I'm powder.

Next a few hundred of me are in a scoop and enjoying a steam bath courtesy of the coffee maker.

I'm liquid now, what will I be, a classic or one of those pretentious creamy tops and who will buy me? I check the queue, please not the guy with the beard, I couldn't stand to be filtered through that growth. To think I could end up as a beard moisturiser.

Me and the clones breathe a sigh of relief it's the cyclist, could have been worse, at least he is clean shaven.

I'm now in a cup, at least it's not one of those plastic take away things and what's next, milk and froth, excellent, I've always wanted to be a cappuccino. On the tray I go along with spoon and napkin, this guy has class. Looks like I have company, a croissant and jam preserve have joined the tray, he grabs the newspaper and off to the table we go.

I sit on the front page of the Times, moved occasionally as he reads a story on the rising price of me. Next I suffer from flakes of pastry falling from each bite that he takes of the croissant. Come on mate I'm getting cold, it's been five minutes now and the froth has gone. Whoops here we go cup to mouth and down the hatch. Whoosh! It's like the big dipper at Blackpool Pleasure Beach.

All sorts of gurgling and bubbling going on down here,

"*Bonjour Arabica,*" its Frenchie the croissant who came down before me along with John the Jam from Lancashire.

John nods "*Ow do lads, won't be long now*" and with that he and Frenchie disappear!

What did he mean by that, "*Won't be long now*"?

I wonder where the next part of this journey will take me?

17. The Thirty Somethings.

The seating outside the café is now full of the new generation drinking coffee and inhaling Bank Holiday traffic CO_2 emissions in equal proportion, same as the silver bikers, nothing changes.

That's how this story ends so what happened leading up to that final paragraph?

The silver bikers have been usurped by the new generation who have registered my favourite coffee spot as their preferred stopping off point for their weekend jaunts.

So it is, that the leader of this group arrives first and is standing at the counter in front of the barista ready to order. At this point he chooses to phone the rest of the team to find out where they are and takes their order for coffee. "Can't hear you," he bellows. "Must be a bad reception area, hang on I'll go outside."

Turning to the barista. "Hold on one second mate." Mate? One thing this barista isn't is his mate. That's evident from the look on his face as team leader walks outside leaving barista and by now several customers waiting his return.

There is a new confidence in this generation, a new level of alpha male that seem incapable of holding a conversation within normal decibel levels. Whether it's on the phone, one to one or ordering drinks they bark out their opinions. Or maybe I'm going deaf. (see chapter, "If it's good enough for Neil Armstrong.")

So, life is put on hold waiting for team leader to return, and I am left wondering why we exercise such patience, maybe it's the nature of the older generation, are we too polite?

By now the guy in the middle of the queue has had enough. "Sod this for a game of soldiers, I'm off to Costa," and with that he hot foots it down the road in the vain hope of securing his caffeine shot quicker than the rest of us, who, by now, are considering the virtues of instant coffee, at home. We all shuffle forward one place.

Team leader returns with the rest of the crew and there's no lycra on display emphasising bumps and lumps, all are finely tuned thirty somethings. However, their shorts have a rather noticeable padded seat which makes one think the occupier has endured an unfortunate accident in their pants. Check this out when next you see a group of riders, although do be careful as they might think you bit weird checking their derriere.

Manufacturers like Raleigh and Dawes have been replaced with Fuji, Roux t7 and the wonderfully named Cinelli Gazzette Della Strada. These mobile pieces of art are extremely light in weight, made almost exclusively from carbon fibre, a far cry from the metal Raleigh with spoked wheels of the 1960's.

Their proud owners have anchored them to anything that is either cemented into the ground or a tree outside the café. Not surprising when you consider the price of these desirable modes of transport, many costing as much as a small car, however, requiring no road tax or insurance. Something I find a tad irritating, considering the proliferation of bicycles on the road and provision of special cycle lanes, paid for by my road tax!

Much to the relief of the other customers various blends of coffee are ordered and dispersed throughout the team. Their conversation, all done at speed, refers to where they have been, several local towns are mentioned, travel times are compared, and hazards encountered en-route. The latter involves various disparaging remarks, mostly about motorist although the humble pedestrian doesn't get away scot free, "Walking into our cycle lanes," shouts the leader, emphasising the word our.

Feeling a little judgemental I muse that they are probably drivers themselves of high-powered Audi, BMW or Mercedes. Which reminds me of the proverb, 'people in glass houses' etc, etc. Realising I'm no better, let's move on.

They exit the premises and the noise level in the shop plummets, sighs of relief can be heard as civilised levels of conversation emerge.

The seating outside the café is now full of the new generation drinking coffee and inhaling Bank holiday traffic CO2 emissions in equal proportion, same as the silver bikers, nothing changes.

18. A Ripping Yarn

Until recently I felt quite sorry for the young people I encountered wearing Jeans that were ripped, sometimes in several places. Such a shame they couldn't afford to have them repaired, buy an inexpensive pair from Matalan at £10.99p or the local charity shop for less.

It was only when I noticed their accessories that I began to question my earlier feelings. Gucci shoes, handbags by Hermes and the exposed skin was not an anaemic pale white, no, it was more of an orange tan that appeared from the opening of the jean.

Young mums with prams - like army trucks - and cheeky chaps congregate in the coffee shop wearing what I now know is the fashion and for the benefit of the more cultured sartorial reader, I use the word 'fashion' loosely.

There are a variety of split jeans on show from the minor tear on the hip, to the full blooded multi slits – the Freddy Kruger cut - leaving very little denim on view. In addition, we have on display boxer shorts in a light mustard colour curtesy of a guy whose jean is split across the right cheek of his derriere. The contrast mustard with the blue denim is, I must confess quite fetching.

The most adventurous designs are those worn by the young mums, in one case a mere simple thread seemed to be the only life line of the bottom half of the jeans to its other half above the knee.

So, here we are again in a wealthy Cheshire market town with the young things wearing their £300 designer jeans, yes, I did say £300, check it out for yourself. It seems the more rips and hence less material the greater the price. I leave you to work out the logic behind that one for yourselves.

By way of comparison, if you were to travel ten miles down the road to the less affluent parts of Manchester, then you will find people wearing jeans in a similar condition however, for different reasons than the stylish Cheshire set. These are not designer cut, their's are worn and torn through countless nights of rough sleeping on the City streets.

As is usual in these stories there is an element of reminiscing and this tale is no exception.

Here we go. I can remember in the early sixties, that's 1960, the rage was for a pair of Levi Strauss jeans, copper riveted. The only place one could buy them was at the Army & Navy store in Piccadilly. The recommended action was to purchase a pair at least one size too big then on arriving home, wear jeans and run a cold bath, sit in said bath for twenty minutes or as near to that time as one could stand the cold. The material was known to shrink, and this self-abuse was to ensure one ended up with a pair that fit perfectly.

It always worked, although the early denim was like canvass and sometimes needed a couple of cold baths to reduce them in size to the required fit. Which was then followed by a severe cold and a week off school.

Why, I hear you ask did you not just put the jeans in the water and why cold? That's what any normal person would do, however we were fourteen and gullible, neither can I recall asking at the time nor if we received a reasonable answer.

If todays ripped jean had been the fashion of the 60's (1960) I am sure we would have gone to M&S (Marks and Spencer) and used a pair of scissors to create our own individual style.

Not these days when you can buy them abused and damaged by the manufacturer for £300!

19. What's in a Name?

"Lola." That was the name the barista shouted above the noise, thus announcing the arrival of one fudge latte' special.

"Here," came the reply from the young woman waiting at the dispensing end of the long coffee counter.

I had an immediate flashback to my days at Failsworth Boys School and the deputy head Reginal Turner barking out the morning attendance register in regimental fashion. Only then our reply was accompanied with an obligatory, "Sir."

After collecting her drink Lola moved to set up office at one of the tables offering Wi-Fi facilities, leaving half a dozen caffeine junkies in her wake. Still waiting on their order, the early signs of withdrawal symptoms were beginning to set in. Fidgeting, muttering and fiddling with their mobile phones, all signs that the irritation of having to wait was taking its toll.

Over the past few months I had visited Manchester on several occasions, which presented me with an opportunity for trying other brands of the 'bean', from Fair Trade to the Corporates on the high street. All this in the name of my investigative journalism and research looking for new stories from the unsuspecting office workers around central Manchester. Their gossip was my bread and butter and metaphorically speaking, I had been served up a feast. Today was no exception and here I was in a queue of a Corporate coffee establishment, the brand of which has a connection with Moby Dick and Captain Ahab.

I thought my tolerance to noise in these places had been well tested due to my status as a regular at the local coffee shop in deepest Cheshire. It was in this training ground where I was exposed to the WI meetings, dogs barking and the full-on orchestra of a baby creche recital accompanied by young mums gossiping, all whilst having my daily coffee. However, nothing could have prepared me for the volume that had greeted me as I entered the shop a few minutes earlier. It was as though someone had suddenly turned the volume to MAX, with decibels on steroids. Each group of busy patrons seemed as though they were trying to out shout those on the next table.

Smartphone ringtones of Mamma Mia, Beyoncé and the annoying simulated telephone bell were bursting out all over the place. Conversations ranged from a guy on his mobile trying to buy an iPad from Apple. Whilst talking with 'Betsy' in the States – who seemed very patient – he broadcast to everyone else in a ten-mile radius his entire bank details, sort code, account number and what I assume were the last three digits of this credit card.

Others were huddled in small groups on conference calls, like the one with Billy Wang from Hong Kong who was quoting the latest company performance stats to his colleagues and anyone else who cared to listen. All this coupled with the hissing coffee machines, baristas shouting orders and the piped music, curtesy of the Bee Gees was enough for me to consider action to preserve my sanity.

Why not jump up on a chair and shout ,"Stop you're all nuts"! In hindsight I don't think it would have made any difference. They would probably have carried on regardless, at best paused for a second to register this lune stood on a chair, then resumed normal service.

For the record I resisted any temptation. Or in other words 'bottled it!'

Back to the queue I was now part of.

There is a long counter and moving left to right, one orders, pays the barista then moves down to the far end where drinks are made and dispensed. During this process I hear the barista asking customers, who were ahead of me, their name then writing this on the take away cup. This part of the process had been adopted to ensure those waiting at the dispensing end of the counter would be certain of receiving their named and correct order.

When it came to my turn, I ordered my usual brew and for some reason when asked for my name I replied, "Maxwell." Don't ask me why, maybe it was the devilment in me, anyhow the barista noted this name on the cup, which is now in their system. Back at the dispensing end, coffees of all types arrive for Jan, Ben and Em. Then I hear, "Max." This didn't immediately register with me as I had given the name Maxwell. Then everyone in the queue started to look at each other, you know that, 'Don't look at me, it's not mine, is it yours?' glance, without actually saying anything.

Realising it's me, I shout, "Here Sir!" Whoops. That caused a moment of rare hilarity from the room. There must be others present who remembered Reginald, or Reg as we called him, but not to his face.

For the next half hour, I go through the alphabet of names and find very few, although Harold works, that we Brits wouldn't shorten when in discussion with the owner. Try it for yourself, the nearest I got was Horatio and there hasn't been one of those since 1805!

Consequently, over the next few weeks I put my findings to the test, mascaraing as Archibald (Archie), Donaldson (Don), Leonardo (Leo) and Simon (Si). There was not one occasion when the plastic cup arrived with the name I had given, all were abbreviated as above in brackets.

So, I design a 'Baldrick style' cunning plan. Come the day of the test, I order coffee, and Barista asks for my name to which I reply, "Costa." Without missing a heartbeat she writes Costa on the cup and we are in the system. To be fair these baristas are on autopilot and particularly, in a busy city centre shop, they hardly have time to catch a breath.

I watch, 'Cup Costa' on its journey down the production line, firstly a one shot of coffee, then the milk and finally the foam is gently coaxed on top. I'm in position at the distribution point, ahead of me I hear names being called. Firstly Will, next is Oli then Josh who each collect their coffees. Next up is me and I hear……

Now there are four possible outcomes to this tale. Consider those below and you decide which one, if any, actually happened.

A. Barista shouts, "OK who's the wise guy"?   **Rumbled**
B. Barista shouts, "Costa" when looking for the purchaser. There's a short silence then uproar and laughter as the irony sinks in?   **Result**
C. Barista shouts "Costa" and no one bats an eyelid. The masses carry on their high-octane conversations?   **Failure**
D. Cup arrives without a name and I must claim my nameless cappuccino?   **Damp squid**

To be continued.

20. Double Standards

On entering my favourite caffeine dispensary, usually a place of tranquillity and relaxation, I am faced with my worst nightmare. Well, not exactly. Shopping in the Arndale centre on a hot Saturday afternoon, appearing on I'm a Celebrity or Stretford Rangers winning the title would be worse.

On this occasion it's a queue at the counter seven deep and most have brought their canine friends who insist on sniffing one another (the dogs that is) a most disturbing sight before breakfast.

I decide that drastic action is called for, consequently accepting there will be repercussions. I plant my bag, newspaper and coat on the best chair in the place, the chesterfield leather sofa, then re-join the end of the queue. Territorial rights have been established, its mine so keep off! Immediately I can feel the eyes of those in front, who had their sights set on the same seat, drilling into me.

I have knowingly committed a major sin, a breach in etiquette. Something that I have commented on as a selfish act when performed by others who have yet to order their daily fix.

Being British, those in the queue retain a degree of silence relying on passive annoyance with mutterings of discontent. Eye contact is made through furrowed brows and levelled in my direction. I have turned those in front of me into a simmering mob who are now actively glancing around for alternative accommodation to suit them and their canine friends.

Double standards it may be, and I plead guilty, however, today I am in need of a comfortable seat in which to lose myself in journalistic waffle.

By now the place is full and there on the ground floor near the window, with the best street view and the benefit of the air conditioning is my chair, waiting for the latest occupier, once my coffee arrives.

21 "You cannot be serious!"

Somewhat tired of the tea and various coffees on sale in the high street, I decided to experiment and make my own version.

My recipes include, the mustard and marmite teas, literally didn't go down to well. The coffee through a hollowed-out asparagus used as a straw, was a disaster.

A similar fate was in store for my spice tea consisting of a normal tea bag with salt and pepper. Whatever else you may try do not go for a cappuccino with prosecco instead of milk, it is not what you might be hoping for.

I have always enjoyed a good relationship with Bill, our postman. Consequently, on seeing him approach with this day's load of marketing material, I decided to offer him the unique experience of being the first to taste my latest potion. I explained my new brewing experiment to Bill, and he was keen to get involved. Handing him a mug of my latest offering he asks about the ingredients. I get as far as, "coffee and soya," at which point he takes a good mouthful. Then hears me complete the sentence with, "sauce."

"You cannot be serious," he exclaims. "Coffee and soya sauce"!

He had assumed this to be coffee made with soya milk. How wrong can you be?

Since then our regular daily greetings have ceased as he moves quickly on to the next house with his bundle of brown envelopes, flyers for Stena Stair Lifts and Iceland Groceries.

My final offering to my family was the teacobovrila, which I thought sounded very continental and interesting - yes, its tea and Bovril - however it just made everyone sick.

I have now run out of guinea pigs for my experiments, alienating Bill and my family in the process.

So, as a last resort I decide to take my own medicine and have one last go at producing the alternative beverage to tea and coffee. I combine the two, great idea I say to myself, obvious!

The recipe is, one tea bag in a mug, add boiling water, remove tea bag after 30 seconds, next add half a teaspoon of coffee and stir enthusiastically. I considered calling this Teac off, however that sounded a little offensive so Cofftea it is.

Verdict, well no one is prepared to try it given their previous experiences and I must admit it is an acquired taste.

Next, experimenting with corn flakes!

Book Two - Italy 2017

1. Out and About - From Chelford to Pogerola

Lessons learnt during the holiday in Italy. May to June 2017

Firstly, it would be useful to explain the manner of my entry into Italy. Somehow, I managed inadvertently, I may add, to use Moi's passport at the EU automatic control point to enter Naples! It gets even more bizarre because then realising I had her passport I had to somehow return it so she could enter. In an action more associated with ten pin bowling, I slide the passport in full view of all the officials and other passengers along the floor until she was able to retrieve same. On placing passport on the scanner, the barcode registered, she too was in. Consequently, I am not officially in the country however, Moi is here in duplicate.

Our departure will be an experience to look forward to, either we depart back to the UK or a prolonged stay at a detention centre awaits us for false entry.

So, reflecting on the holiday, the following are a collection of some *helpful hints, warnings which I hope you will find useful and Do's and Don'ts* when negotiating a purchase at a local shop or paying a bill in a restaurant, none of which you will find on Trivago or other travel web sites.

1. Don't Use a €50 note when buying milk (price €1.20), this upsets shopkeepers who go loco trying to find all that Euro change.

2. Don't Help an older citizen, seniora, with her shopping. They think you are trying to mug them and complain in language so intense it would strip paint off the walls. Leave quickly before the Polizia arrive.

3. Do wave your arms about like a whaling ban-chi during a conversation, it makes one feel Italian and they like it.

4. Use the phrase 'Prego' all the time, it's a word for any occasion.

5. The euro notes look like Monopoly money, so be aware of the various denominations and in particular, slight variation in colours. Easy to make a mistake and give a twenty euro tip when five euros would suffice. Once in the waiters hands it's gone!

6. Queuing is pointless, they don't understand the concept, particularly when the bus arrives. I suggest the method taught to me by Emily. It's called the 'Wisconsin Elbows' approach. On putting this into action you will notice it's the tourists who are not used to this and back off in surprise. The locals are the ones you need to be positive with. Ignore their protestations and just shout 'Prego.' (see item 4 above)

7. The local motorists here are nuts, seriously. They are only surpassed in their kamikaze style driving by motorcyclists who insist on overtaking several vehicles at once whilst entering a dark tunnel on a single carriageway, with a passenger on board and texting.

8. Here's an easy one, smile when engaging the locals. They'll think you a little strange at first however, will join in after a day or two.

9. Don't mention Mussolini!

10. Don't mention *Brexitus!*

11. If you want to hire a speed boat for a trip along the coast make sure you emphasise the word speed. Otherwise you will end up on a tuk-tuk traveling at 3 mph and contract sunstroke. Don't expect sympathy, the boat hustlers on the quay side were not granted that gene.

12. If your thirteen-year-old boat guide suggests an inexpensive detour to see the cave pools, be alert, you have been warned. Under the water you will see lots of rock shapes some resembling well known politicians and others garden gnomes, all probably bought from the local equivalent of Aldi.

13. It's obvious now why the Romans built so many flat straight roads in 50 BC when holidaying in Britannica. Contrary to popular belief that this was the quickest way of getting from

A to B, they were in fact just practicing the use of *tarmaticus* for when they returned to Rome. By the way they are still trying to finish the M6!

13. Don't get paranoid, if you think they are talking about you in their own language then they probably are. Just adopt point eight above.

14. Don't be taken in by any smart talking salesperson, male or female, if they don't see an immediate buying sign then you are toast and they move quickly on to the next unsuspecting tourist.

Apart from that we had a really great time.

Footnote. Not wishing to upset our Italian cousins let me say I can only comment on our trip to the Amalfi region, other parts of this beautiful country are probably very different.

2. Rapping in Italy

There are three rappers on the cafe terrace doing their thing, waving their arms and gesticulating with their fingers. Even with their headphones on the 'music' - the jury's still out on that definition - can be clearly heard by the rest of us on the terrace above.

I can safely predict that given the decibels of this 'music,' their eardrums will be toast in a couple of hours let alone any psychological damage that may be inflicted on their brains.

One thing is for sure they will definitely need hearing aids, how cool is that a rapper with hearing aids! Hilarious. Also, a top-class psychologist will be essential.

For my daughter in-law Dr Emily, please note I have their mobile numbers for future business. By the way all three are from the US.

I digress, to continue ...

Sitting in the shade watching are a group of our antipodean friends from Sydney, looks like a Bruce and a couple of Sheila's.

Next to them are an English couple from Harrow.

The 'music' or whatever the rap term is for this creation, gets louder. Fuelled by the odd Fosters or ten, the Aussies shout for more and Bruce and his mates join in. Now fully committed, he, Bruce delights us all in his interpretation of an ageing Aussie rapper, not a pretty site, more like a Kangaroo on steroids.

His nineteenth century deported ancestors must have committed a serious crime, for their genes have certainly passed down the generations to this now whirling dervisher.

The Brits?

They quietly finish their drinks and leave, or if you prefer Brexit.

3. Cosmopolitania.

Italy 2017. Beneto's Restaurant in Pogerola

There are quite a mix of nationalities here at the restaurant in the mountains above the Amalfi coast.

On meeting new people, I have ceased to ask which part of the States they are from, having upset so many of our Canadian commonwealth partners.

There are plenty of representatives from the penal colonies, mostly from Melbourne. I try and engage in a conversation with Bruce and his mates however, he and they are all intent on expressing their views on cricket and 'that Sheila' you have as prime minister. The conversation is one-way traffic with Dundee hardly stopping to take breath, so I wait for an opening when he finishes his 'Larga!'

At this juncture I score two points, firstly I mention ball tampering and secondly, I remind him that one of their recent occupants of that high office was born in Wales. So, take that Boyo!!

Since going to press we have lost the ashes yet scored a moral victory on fair play and interfering with cricket balls and witnessed a tearful news report from their now cricket ex-captain.

Moving on, if you like walking then this is the place to be however, health and safety regs are non-existent. There are plenty of narrow paths snaking down the mountains with no fencing to provide protection from the shear drop. I conclude the last time any maintenance was carried out would have been when Julius Caesar was feeding Christians to the lions at the Coliseum in Rome.

Our Germanic cousins are here in force and look the part with their high viz vests, which make them easier to spot when falling off the high mountain paths. Knapsacks are probably full of Kendal Mint Cake or Knockwurst and those 'walking sticks'? I'm sure it's the 'in thing' to have, however, they look incomplete without the skis.

From all that exercise, one can see how they have developed those huge leg and thigh muscles, the men are much the same as well. Furthermore, one must be in the club to understand the language of these serious walkers. The various hiking boots have specially designed soles and some socks are better than others however, it's Vaseline which is the main subject of today's conversation.

Apparently, it has lubricant qualities which help with chafing in certain areas. The rest of their conversation which goes into detail on the application of this substance to various parts of the human anatomy is too sensitive to report. I do admire their attention to detail, no wonder they are good at taking penalties.

I should add it's only the Germans perfect use of English that allows me to report on these events.

How lazy we Brits have become in learning to communicate with the rest of the world. I should have stayed on an extra year at school and taken languages!

4. HRT and Ben

Passports yes, boarding passes yes, funny money yes, you know what it's like. Four o'clock in the morning and you're wondering why you booked the early flight!

The house is now in lockdown and we are bleary-eyed waiting for a taxi to arrive at some ungodly hour. The memory of that last thirty minutes of sleep which one eventually found, before the alarm torpedoed one's slumber, lingers until we hear the taxi pull up outside.

There is nothing worse than a talkative driver at 04:05hrs in the morning. Go on, admit it please, how can he be so awake? I know it's the exorbitant fee I am paying him for this ride, but why does he feel he has to entertain me with stories of previous passengers?

Airport, flight, arrive, taxi, hotel.... we are here it's 2 pm the same day and we have arrived, hallelujah, collapse on the bed and sleep. No, that's a bad idea, best try and keep to a normal sleep pattern.

One bottle of Prosecco supplemented by fresh orange juice later and all is well with the world.

Anyhow, that's how the first day of our long-awaited trip to Italy started. We had planned this for months and accounted for everything. Next day beautiful sunshine, hot as if one had opened an oven door on full heat; we had arrived. Unpack now? No, what the hell! Time for a cappuccino and croissant, the first of many over the next few weeks.

You know that point when you actually believe everything is going right and then God in his wisdom decides it's about time you learned another lesson? Well as you will have guessed, that moment has just arrived.

Returning to the apartment I find my other half, Moi routing through the suitcases and asking me if I have seen her patches?

What are we talking about? Explanation.......

We are talking about HRT patches, the givers of life, they are nowhere to be found. Accusations of irresponsibility are flying to and fro. Suitcases are turned inside out, upside down, pockets are checked and rechecked, nothing. Hostilities are about to break out when we realise we have left them at home.

Let me say to our credit, there is no further evidence of panic, sanity prevails as we consider the consequences and action open to us. Phone the GP at home, of course they will send a prescription and we can buy them here in Italy, after all we are still members of the EU and there must be some form of reciprocal arrangement in place.

Several phone calls later to our GP and we are no further forward. We might as well be phoning from outer Siberia and asking for heroin, no help at all.

So, off to Amalfi we go to find a pharmacy. As a 'fail safe' we phone Ben in Sheffield -that's my son and heir - who kindly drives from Sheffield to our home, forty miles away and sure enough finds the said 'patches' on the hall table. He sends them to us first class registered post on the Monday.

You still with me?

Meanwhile, back in Amalfi, Moi is engaged in a conversation with the pharmacist explaining our plight. "No patches, left at Casa in Britannica." She makes her point however; the pharmacist proceeds to deliver a lecture on why they cannot provide said items without a prescription. We are told to find a local doctor who will issue the required document but, only after he/she has spoken with our GP in the UK! After much pleading and gesticulation the pharmacists agrees to sell said 'patches' on a mercy prescription, whatever that is. We are just glad to have the things and head to the bar.

Now we move forward to the Friday and still nothing has arrived from the UK. The patches from Amalfi are only half strength so Moi is having to double up on them covering two legs. So much so that over two legs they make a reasonable checker board.

To be clear, not two legs as in a football match but her legs side by side resemble a chequer board with all the patches as the squares. Well, take away the castle and bishop and you could have a reasonable game of chess on both legs. Although the king keeps disappearing when she moves.

It's the following Monday and still nothing from the UK so off we go to Amalfi only this time we find a different pharmacy, convinced the original one wouldn't be so obliging this time.

Pharmacy number two, Moi explains the situation and just as the pharmacist is about to announce the problem, I hear, "Excuse me." Woops! Heard that tone before. What ensues is Madam telling the pharmacist that she knows all about the regulations and prescription requirements, however, we are English. (note; English not British, love it when we are specific about our heritage) and this is not what Maggie Thatcher or Ted Heath signed up for, we expect more *entente cordial.* So will she please find the appropriate medication and dispense it immediately.

We leave the premises with the patches.

The elusive patches finally arrived from the UK ten days after posting, by which time Moi was looking more like a patchwork quilt.

5. Juan Manuel Fangio

This guy was a driving legend in his own life time. Google him, it will save me time explaining how he made history in what is now Formula 1 grand prix racing.

He 'drove' the car, used manual gears with a stick shift that looked more like a walking stick and a hand brake, yes hand break, on the outside of the driver's side. There was no such thing as 'automatic this, that and the other' as in modern cars. For example his driving wheel was more like a cartwheel in size and his crash helmet no more than a Heinz beans tin. His cavalier attitude and great skill took him to five world championships, and he achieved numerous other records.

So, why am I labouring on about an Argentinian legend from the 1950s and 60's when reporting from Italy in 2017? Here's the thing. We are about to board the local bus from Pogerola to Amalfi, which by the way is some two thousand meters above sea level, and I am looking forward to a casual yet, knowing my better half, not inexpensive tour around the local shops.

Our driver is a short guy about fifty years of age with typical Roman features of nose and jet black yet, receding hair line. He perspires a lot; trust me I know, I am down wind of him.

The descent is fine for the first ten meters, then the driver, let's call him Juan, takes total control of the road. This is his space, and no one will either overtake or win in a head-to-head standoff. The narrow road zig zags down the mountain, no white centre lines to separate the oncoming traffic. Cornering is like a personal challenge between Juan and the laws of physics, he wins. Not sure how, as the Mediterranean seems to be our next destination as he takes each corner at high speed and somehow manages to snake the long single decker bus around the tightest of corners.

Oncoming traffic means nothing to Juan, whether automotive or human, [It]needs to move out of his way. Incredibly, buses coming up the road manage to pass us by millimetres and one can easily see the look of fear in the eyes of the other passengers as window meets window. I can only assume Juan must be related to the other drivers and madness runs in the family.

Reference my opening paragraphs, this is Juan Fangio reincarnated as our bus driver.

Approaching each bend in the road, he bears down on the horn, alerting those unfortunate souls around the corner of his pending arrival or their doom. He wins each time as the oncoming traffic remains stationary deferring to his arrival. Eventually he must stop due to the traffic cop in the road. Obeying the halt sign Juan waits his turn then off we go again.

What seemed like a lifetime is only twenty minutes and we arrive in Amalfi safe and sound. Not sure about sound, grateful is probably the word I would use.

On alighting from the bus, I, for some unknown reason turn and say, "Great drive, Juan," who uncannily replies, "Grazie," with a huge grin on his face.

He wins!

6. Breakfast on Coffee and Croissant

It's one of those warm sunny mornings when the sky is bright MCFC blue and I have just completed a fifteen-minute conversation with a lovely Italian lady, during which I attempted to order my morning coffee and croissant.

I know what you're thinking, and you are right, it shouldn't take that long however, neither of us speaks the other's language. This is not an insurmountable problem, but we strive to make it one.

She, smiling and waving arms whilst talking at a tremendous speed, me speaking in English and employing an Italian accent!!

I mean how stupid is that, as if she will understand me any better as I ask for,

" A coffa anda a crossando, per favour."

In the end I find myself using bits of French, Spanish and German to complete the order.

That went well!!

I will probably end up with sangria and a knockwurst sausage on a Baguette.

She walks away to the kitchen from which I hear thunderous and constant laughter as she interprets my continental order to her compatriots who seem to find the whole episode hilarious.

Book Three – Italy 2018

1. A Whiter shade of pale - Italy Ravello June 2018

It's just over twelve months since we took the local blue bus from Pogerola situated high in the mountains down to Amalfi.

You may have read my account of that journey in the chapter 'Juan Manuel Fangio', the name I christened our driver that day due to his skill in negotiating the hairpin bends at speed and delivering us safely at our destination.

Today, one year on, we are at the bus station in Amalfi, waiting with other hopefuls for the blue bus that will deliver us to Ravello. Its late, no surprise there then. Locals, Americans, Brits and other members of the EU – we have not yet left that august institution - all congregate out of the sun, under the bus shelter and heave a sigh of relief when our transport arrives.

What follows is a wave of nations, completely out of control charging the door to our transport. At this crucial point the driver informs these would be boarders to "indietro" which roughly translated means, "back off." "Passengers must be allowed to disembark first," he shouts with accompanying hand gestures.

That done we cram the entrance, no quarter given as manners are replaced with elbows. The locals are fine, they are used to this cattle market atmosphere, it's the tourists who seem to lose all self-control and cuss in a verity of languages, pushing and shoving their way to the front.

On the other hand, we Brits form an orderly queue. How stupid is that? Two people in a queue of their own at the back of this mob. I decide enough is enough and employ the 'Emily tactics,' elbows are extended and with Moi firmly holding on to my M&S pants, we're off scything through the EU. This is Brexit in action. Now I am at the front, in my wake are a large number of disgruntled tourists. I stand aside, and Moi jumps on the bus quickly followed by yours truly. Then the driver closes the doors!

That did nothing to improve our relationship with other EU members as those left behind make signs of disapproval at the driver. He, seems completely oblivious to their protestations, merely shouts back, "pieno," "pieno," which I believe is Italian for 'full.' Its standing room only for me and several others. Moi is offered a seat by a polite American guy, which makes me thing he might have witnessed my 'Em-tactics' and approved.

We sway back and forth as the driver manoeuvres his bus up and along the winding narrow road, the blue waters of the Mediterranean coming ever closer each time we take a bend. The tourists are easy to spot, bursting into fits of nervous laughter each time we have a near miss with oncoming traffic, a brick wall or a maniac on a scooter. On the other hand, the locals sit quietly either totally engaged with their mobile phone or chatting to their neighbour.

It's about halfway into the journey that I become conscious of the speed at which Manuel Jr is propelling this blue bullet at; an alarming rate of knots, without moving out of second gear. So, to recap, we are travelling up steep hills, rolling around in this packed airless metal container, inches away from the cliff edge at 30kph and ready to meet our maker at any second.

Fast forward twenty minutes. Son of Fangio has delivered us all safe to Ravello. I have mixed feelings of relief, yes, that's a strong feeling, satisfaction and pride that we have survived, as I notice my fellow travellers do. This then descends into arrogance when I hear comments, "that was easy," "we'll do that again," and the obligatory, "no problem."

Well, you weren't thinking that ten minutes ago, when the orange tan had drained from your face and left you looking like a whiter shade of pale matie.

I turn to see Manuel Jr speeding downhill with a new load of naïve passengers on the return journey. Shortly they will start to question their mortality, "Have I made a will?" "Did I turn the gas off before leaving home?"

I have no doubts he will deliver them safe to Amalfi, however, maybe not quite as sound of mind as they were before boarding his bus.

2. "Cabin Crew to Doors" (Italy Ravello June 2018)

Now the holiday can begin, the waiting is over, we've endured the indignity of the 'senior box scanner,' including a personal body search by an over enthusiastic security guard. All necessary in my case when the 'junior scanner' registered a metal object on my person.

For the record I had forgotten to place my phone in the security tray, hence the red flashing lights when walking through 'junior', which lead to the more intrusive search. Two agitated security guards later and I was allowed 'airside' and mutterings could be heard from those passengers behind me in the queue of 'thoughtless' and 'typical'.

Now if you need perfume, clothing or duty-free booze then this is the place to be. In half an hour one could end up smelling like a tart's boudoir and as drunk as a skunk dressed in all the latest fashion labels, with no chance of boarding the plane!

However, try finding a bathroom or a coffee and sandwich for under twenty pounds and your screwed. Also, why when I visit WH Smith to buy a newspaper do I hear a recording of a lady asking to see my boarding pass? I'm not buying Givenchy perfume, it's a sixty pence purchase for heaven's sake. So as instructed I remove my item from the bagging area at which point the alarm is activated. Lady supervisor arrives and with one swish of her magic card releases me from WHS.

By the way, that's the second alarm I've triggered, and we haven't even left the ground yet.

The information board is now showing our flight number and we are advised to make our way to gate 07 to prepare for boarding. That's easy enough, however what follows, was, in hindsight predictable. The race is now on as an assortment of families, luggage and screaming children are dragged and this is important, at speed towards gate 07.

We are left in a now almost deserted seating area, what's the rush? We saunter off to join the hoards, arriving at the end of the queue still some forty deep. In front of us are a group of Geordies chattering nervously about their drive down from Newcastle and the need for a drink.

Moving on.

"Cabin crew to doors." Here we go, crammed in like sardines, overhead lockers are packed above my seat with everyone's luggage except mine. This pilot isn't messing around, he's either a race junkie or missing his take-off slot might result in him losing his weekly bonus. Short ride to the end of the runway, quick handbrake turn, and we are off. Full throttle, up we climb, ears pop, we level out and relax. Well that was the plan, remember those noisy Geordies? They are seated directly behind us, three hours of this!

If you haven't pre-booked [it] then forget [it] and the stewards don't want to know you. All those who have, are served food, drinks, blankets and water first, ok fair enough. The rest of us will have to wait and wait we do, until we are halfway over the Alps before the steward asks, "Can I get you anything"? Not even a sir or madam, you have to pre-book that level of courtesy. I am tempted to answer, "Is there anything left," but no, I am on holiday, the Geordies are comatose after a lunch of vodka and brown ale, so all is good.

'Oh, Monarch how we miss you?'

Somewhere over Rome at 35000 feet the queue for the bathroom starts to form. Well bathroom is a slight exaggeration, you need to be under five-foot-tall and less that eight stone, then you might be able to enter the cubical. Once inside this will induce the feeling of claustrophobia and a need to exit asap. Over the next half an hour the queue grows steadily, as soon as one poor ashen faced claustrophobic exits another contestant enters. Time is up, we are about to begin our descent into Naples and on instructions from the steward, the remaining half a dozen at the 'loo queue,' are forced to return to their seats. Serves them right for pre-booking all those drinks.

Over the intercom we are told to, "Please remain seated with your seat belt securely fastened until the plane has landed and the captain.............................." The rest is drowned out by passengers retrieving their luggage from overhead lockers and then all are sandwiched in a queue the length of the centre aisle. I swear as this is happening we are still doing ninety mph on the runway, then brakes on, reverse engines, landed.

We arrive early, that's the pilots bonus banked this week, and the stairs to disembark are still not here. Consequently, those standing occupying the aisle must wait, having all shuffled towards the front of the plane they are now unable to return to their seats. Five minutes goes by, how smug we still seated feel, occasionally glancing at the now hot and frustrated line of chancers, such schadenfreude.

And so, to baggage claim gate 07, same as Manchester. Another ten minutes wait and the only activity we have is a four-year-old running around on the stationary luggage conveyor belt. If that were to suddenly start she would be off through the exit and back on the plane to Manchester before realising what had happened. Just in time parent of said child arrives to remove 'at risk' infant who, in her best Mancunian shrieks her disapproval.

Orange lights flash and the conveyor slowly starts to eject the various coloured assortment of bags, cases and skies! En masse we all take two steps forward crossing the blue line so as not to miss our precious cargo the first time around. One guy tries to hoist his bag off the conveyor, however his refusal to let go and the momentum of the belt, results in him chasing his case around the carousel knocking into a couple of innocent by standers en-route. Hilarious, you had to be there.

Hurrah, our cases are in sight, I can now relax in the knowledge that I have a change of clothing. Much to my astonishment Moi leans over and in one movement hoists her bag straight off the conveyor. That's shown the tattooed Geordie boys standing around how to do it. Then, just in case they missed her weight lifting skills first time around, she retrieves our other case with equal dexterity.

Out through the 'arrivals' door and we are faced with a crowd of drivers all holding up name boards. That's our guy with the MR FRANK on a red board. Giuseppe flashes a Colgate smile, three-piece suit, short jacket, jet black hair and olive skin, what's not to like?

For the next two hours, yes two hours, we are driven in a comfortable Mercedes people carrier to our destination. Giuseppe's English is on par with my Italian, so we have a fractured conversation full of gesticulations, bits of Spanish and French thrown in for good measure.

It's now 8.30pm and we have arrived at the Hotel Parsifal. Antonio is there to greet us, let the holiday begin.

Book Four - The Trilogy

1. JV and Me 1959.

The Field

Jim thinks we first met when we were nine or ten years of age at St. John's Junior School after he had moved from Beswick to Failsworth. Had he only known then that Beswick would be the location of the MCFC Etihad stadium 60 years later and me that the pitch would be directly above Bradford Colliery, where my dad worked as a miner.

My earliest memories are playing football on the field facing his parents shop. Straight home from school and on to the field with a ball, any type would do plastic, tennis or occasionally a 'Casie,' more of which later.

The route to the pitch from my home at 21 West Street was as follows:

'Out of front door across road, down a ginnel between two rows of terraced houses. The ginnel, no more than eight feet across was made up of cobbled stones with grass and the odd weed sprouting from cracks between the cobles. All the back-yard gates were wooden, painted the same and only colour available at that time, black creosote. Rubbish bins were the old metal type, one per household. These appeared every Friday morning at the back gates for the binmen to heave over their shoulders and empty into the bin-lorry. No recycling then, there was no need, packaging and Amazon hadn't been invented.

The end of the ginnel opened onto Cow Lane across from which were wooden garages made from burnt timber, and behind them lay 'the field.'

I say field, it was a deserted space of land, a few hundred yards or so across, overgrown with weeds and 'bogs' (a name we christened them). 'Bogs' are a crater filled with water often 12' across and dangerous, as I was later to find out.

Jim lived in a flat above his parents' greengrocers shop and from the first floor one had a panoramic view of the field. There were three other shops, a grocer, butcher and a hardware store, all family run businesses. When he wasn't helping his dad in the shop he was usually first on the field, soon to be joined by several others and when we had enough, the coats would go down at each end to represent the goals. No referee or linesmen, we just made a centre circle, roughly where we thought half way was and kicked off. The ground was so uneven it was like playing on a freshly ploughed field and ball control was nigh impossible.

Many a pair of school shoes were ruined during this time and cuts and bruises were viewed as a badge of honour. Corners, penalties and goals scored were usually decided by the majority vote, very democratic at such a young age.

About 5.30pm the call would come from various parents, ranging from, "*Peter your teas on the table,*" to the dreaded and embarrassing, "*John time for a bath.*"

Jim and I were usually the last to go, not that we were neglected by our parents, we were just doing what we dreamed of, mates playing football. Eventually we were ordered in for tea, however, no sooner had the last chip disappeared from the plate than we and the others assembled again.

This time there might be more playing and at times we were joined by Jim senior, Jim's dad. He wasn't a tall man, slight in build and at 39 years of age he was, to us, old. However, on the pitch no quarter was expected or given. He would run and slide in on tackles like a good 'un. Never heard him curse or get annoyed, he just looked and sounded like he had escaped for a while and during that game he was one of us, one of the boys.

Occasionally we were also joined by Michael. He was a little older than us and had to wear a heavy metal brace on his right leg which provided support from his ankle to his hip. This brace, or callipers as they were called then, was held in place by wide leather straps and must have been extremely heavy and painful, which resulted in his ungainly limp.

Whenever he joined us we all wanted him on our side. It was a fearsome sight to face Michael hobbling down the wing and amazingly within the confines of those iron callipers, in full control of the ball. If you were foolish enough to tackle him then those callipers could really hurt.

To us he wasn't disabled, he was from our area, went to the same school and loved his football. He was just one of the lads.

The 'casie' referred to earlier was a proper football of the type used by professionals. Made of several pieces of leather sewn together and inside was a bladder or inner tube which one inflated using a bicycle pump. The opening was then laced together as one would with a shoe. Maintenance was necessary to keep the leather from hardening, where dubbin, a form of oily leather preservative was applied and then vigorously polished using 'elbow grease.'

In the dry weather this was the perfect ball for the game. The only drawback was after heading the ball, if you caught the lacing then you would have a barcode imprinted on one's forehead for hours afterwards.

However, in the rain, the leather absorbed the water and unless one was possessed by the spirit of Billy Wright, *see google*, one should avoid heading said ball thereby missing out on minor concussion and a trip to Oldham infirmary.

In the summer it was usually 9.30pm when we were forced to stop play for bad light. Tired but satisfied that for a few hours I had lived the dream and been my hero Bert Trautmann.

Who shall I be tomorrow, David Waggstaffe, Johnny Crossan? No, leave that to Jim. I'll be Bert.

Needless to say, Jim and I were staunch blues from an early age. We would go on to play for the senior school team, he right-half, me left-half and Ancoats Lads Club where we won the Manchester Boys club trophy.

Reference:
Casie. Leather football
Elbow grease. Rubbing the ball hard with a cloth

Ginell. Long narrow passage between back to back terraced houses of the 1950's

Bog. Local name for a crater filled with water.

Bin Lorry. Early 1950's lorry used for waste/rubbish collections.

Billy Wright CBE. Wolverhampton Wanderers and England captain (1950's). For a more modern equivalent think Vinny Jones.

2. Maine Road - Pennies from Heaven.

Date 19th October 1963
K.O 3.0pm
MCFC v Preston North End

It's match day and we are off to watch the boys in sky blue.

Jim and I would often go with his dad, from now on known as
JD, and when he would take Jim's grandad, from here on known
as JGD, to the game.

I would race across to Jim's place and there in front of the shop
was the glorious Ford Transit van. On arrival, Jim and I would
remove all the empty boxes from the back of the van that, in the
early hours of the morning, JD had used to collect groceries from
the Manchester veg' market.

Out would come 'Fyffe' banana boxes, followed by orange
crates, string net sacks which earlier held potatoes and sprouts.

Once cleared we would then pile in the back. No seats, we just
sat on the wheel arch and rolled around like apples in a barrel.

Down Propsall Drive and the first stop to pick up JGD. On
route JD would light up what was to be the first of many 'Park
Drive' cigarettes. A thin blue cloud would find its way to the rear
of the van and this at the age of thirteen was to be our
introduction to passive smoking.

Immediately after collecting JGD, he too would light up,
sometimes 'Park Drive' or occasionally 'Woodbine'. It wasn't
long before the thin cloud became a fog, oxygen was now in short
supply until JD opened the driver's window, not to let air in, but
to eject the remains of the fag.

JD knew all the short cuts to the ground, so it wasn't,
mercifully, long until we arrived. We would be deposited to
make our own way to the Kippax Stand whilst JD and JGD
parked and took up residence in the seated area. "Meet here after

the game and don't be late or you'll be walking home," was our instruction from JD.

Of course, he was joking, however we never chanced testing him on that.

Short queue at the dark scary turnstile which made a metallic clanking noise, like a rusty old gate, as the operator, who was hidden behind a mesh screen took our 1s and 3p in old money. These turnstile operators sat behind their security grills with various piles of coins - just out of reach! - to provide change as needed and there was always a seductive smell of meat pies wafting through the grill.

A programme was sixpence and a luxury, so didn't always have enough funding to buy that and said meat pies. We were never sure about the content of these pies, however; hunger had taken over and they were essential eating.

The Kippax Stand was like a giant Aztec pyramid and we made our way down the steps to pitch level, we just wanted to be as close to the players as we could. These were the days before all seater stadiums. At various levels there were – what they called 'safety barriers' – consisting of metal frames about 6 feet across and 4-foot high which one could lean against. Thirty or so of these were dotted around the Kippax.

Groundsmen emerged, and nets were attached to the goal posts, photographers jostled for the best place, usually behind what they hoped would be the away team's goal. No warm up on the pitch, as they do now. It was 2-55pm, the roar went up and out would come the two teams. Stan Bowles famously stubbing out his fag on the gravel before walking on to the pitch. Hilarious!

No waiting for 'Sky', the ref tossed a coin and ends were chosen by the captains. At 3pm whistle went and off we go, the game plan was simple to score more goals than the opposition, no 4.4.2, or 4.2.4 formations it was 5 forwards, 3 centre and half backs, two full backs and Harry Dowd in goal or if injured then Ken Mulhearn.

Imagine, two boys on their own in amongst thirty thousand other Mancs, and you never felt threatened. There was a feeling of each looking after the other. Older guys, aged 21 upwards, seemed to look out for us and would give up their place so we could get closer to the pitch.

Except on one occasion.

Half way through one match pennies started falling from the sky. This was attributed to several away supporters who had infiltrated the Kippax and from the top of the stand, began raining pennies down on us at the front.

For some reason I managed to avoid these projectiles, however Jim didn't! Although we had much more head hair in those days it wasn't enough protection from these copper missiles. They rained down on him and as I was told at the time they, " ******* hurt"!

At the final whistle we headed off to the meeting place. For those unlucky enough not to have a lift, there were the red Foden buses parked nose to tail, snaking along the front of the ground, twenty or so waiting for either the elated or downhearted supporters.

I always thought it ironic the colour in front of Maine Road was bright red, colour of Stretford Rangers! How annoying.

The return journey was spent either praising the team or a character assassination on the likes of Derek Kevan or Paul Aimson. The latter, "how well he suits his name, neither could hit a barn door with a cows a........!"

Note: Memorable quote from a spectator at the game.

"Where's Cliff Sear going?"

As he failed to tackle the opposing winger and then ran back to his own goals.

"He's off to give Harry Dowd a message." Hilarious!

Jim and I are the only two people who can appreciate the humour, you had to be there.

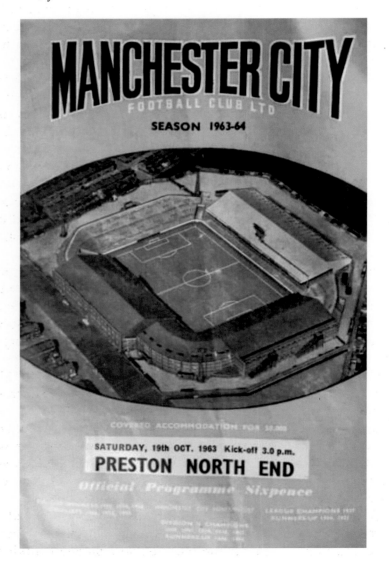

3. 'Fiery Jack'

It's December 1964 and we are through to the semi-finals of the Oldham Athletic Cup. This is the most prestigious of school competitions and so far this year we have won the League and Law Swallow Cup.

We have an away game at Crompton School, arriving early that Saturday morning, we change in their school gymnasium. To say it's cold would be an understatement, the pitch is rock solid and looks like a miniature version of the 'Himalayas'. In local terms its 'Brass Monkey' weather.

For an appreciation of how cold we felt that day try reading the next few paragraphs with your head in the fridge!

Their school caretaker had decided to save coal, so there was no heating in the changing room, nor, as we were to find out later, hot water for the showers. Hence eleven anaemic-looking fourteen-year-olds get changed.

For our kit, we wore black shirts as provided by the school with the badge, FBS on the front left. Shorts and socks were a mixture of black or white. I am guessing, whatever we had been bought for birthday or Christmas presents. Consequently, we never all wore the same, in one game. Pete Dane turned up in Red shorts and Kenny in red socks. See photo below.

Our boots were black with three white stripes down the side and usually 'Adidas', either moulded or detachable studs. Whichever, they were no match for the 'Himalayas'.

Shin pads were an option however, woe-betide anyone who sustained a bang on the shin without wearing them. It was painful in the extreme, only a kick in the nether regions was worse, which most of the lads had experienced on several occasions.

We were a team as good in our day as Real Madrid, di Stefano's Hungary or Brazil well in our minds we thought we were and that's all that mattered. We had a shared confidence that 'Chic' would score goals, 'Steve' would put their centre forward out of action and 'Fred' would dribble the ball and confuse not only the opposition but himself in the process.

The line up on the field with shirt numbers, no such thing as squad numbers then:

[Goal Keeper]
Colin Atkinson (1)

Dave Mitchell (2)   -   Steve Morton (3)

Jim (4) - Kenny (5) - Me (6)

Fred (7) - Chic (8) - Pete Dane (9) - David G' (10) - Barry (11)

In all our time together, I never heard a cross word exchanged, except on that Saturday morning.

Kenny, centre half, was in real agony after unintentionally smearing 'fiery jack' heat cream on his private parts in an attempt to keep warm, poor decision.

This was a cream I had bought to rub into my knee joints, just to warm up the muscles however, Kenny got hold of it and after usage forgot to wash his hands.

Whilst tucking his shirt into his shorts he must have caught other more delicate parts of the male anatomy with this 'fiery jack.' It took almost the first half for him to stop whaling in pain.

We lost the game 1-0 and so ended our dreams of playing at a real football stadium. To say Oldham FC and 'real football stadium' in the same sentence may be somewhat of an oxymoron. They were in the old fourth division at the time and their stadium was a dump. Well that was how we consoled ourselves during our post-match analysis. Although, I'm not sure we knew the word oxymoron existed at that age, after all we were secondary school boys not Grammar school material!

Kenny sustained no lasting damage, I believe he married and went on to have children.

Quote from the day:

Ten minutes into the game, on seeing Kenny running around like a demented frog.

Steve to Kenny in a loud passionate and fearsome voice.

"We're all hurting Kenny"!!

To anyone else it's an innocent sentence without meaning. To Jim and me it was and remains hilarious, you had to be there on that freezing December morning.

Here they are:-

Back row. Steve, me, Bazz, Colin, Mitch, Jim, Pete and Mr Jones.

Front row: Gimbledestin, Chic, Kenny (capt), Fred and Neil (sub)

Post Script:

For those of you who are interested in the finer details and wondering about their goal and how it happened, let me satisfy your curiosity.

I sent a draft of this article to a member of the team just to check the accuracy of my recollections from that day. After fifty-four years it has come to light the individual, who shall remain nameless, - you know who you are- gave away a penalty from which they [Crompton] scored the only goal of the game.

As promised I have not revealed the name of that person, it would be churlish to do so. Enjoy......

PPS: Hope that's OK Jim?

(Everyone see picture, sixth from the left back row !!!!!)

Book Five - Manchester 1966 – 1971 - 1974

1. The Number 98 to Stevenson Square

Let me set the scene for you, it's 1967 and I am one year into my first real job. Well, discounting my final year at school as a part time grocery boy tearing around Failsworth on my delivery bike, similar to the one in the Hovis advert, only I didn't wear a flat cap. Very cool now, however not the head gear for an aspiring 15-year-old in the early 60's.

Following my introduction to the world of work, my initial concerns of arriving late have gone, no longer am I there for 8.30am - official start time 9.00am. I have my transport arrangements into Manchester down to a fine art of catching the late bus and arriving bang on time.

This was not the result of strenuous research of time tables, just my estimate of how long it takes to walk from my home to the bus stop on the main road, from which one boarded the bright red bus to Manchester.

The bus stop consisted of a weather shelter, resembling an upside-down letter L, alongside it stood an eight-foot vertical metal post marked 'To Manchester Centre' and the numbers 98, 82 and 10 printed on a square plaque which hung like a flag in the breeze.

The stop was located on the main road; however, my route involved a short walk along a side street from which one could not see the down town traffic. It was however situated within a few yards of turning the corner onto the main road and my bus stop. I usually arrived within minutes of my favoured 98 bus which would deliver me to Stevenson Square in good time for a ten-minute walk to Deansgate where my employer, Stenhouse Northern were based.

The 82 was my back up, however, this stopped in St Peters Square and involved a longer walk to the office.

Finally, there was the no 10, the Oldham Express. Usually driven by ex-Service men who had previously commanded tanks during their days doing national service and found the express route exhilarating. In order to attract the driver's attention, the prescribed action was to stand in the road and wave one's arms in a manner of a sailor with two table tennis bats trying to park a plane on an aircraft carrier. One began the procedure when the bus was approximately half a mile away to allow sufficient distance for tankman to notice and apply brakes.

On this particular day I was seconds away from turning the corner when the 98 pulled away from the stop, it was early. The bright red Lucas manufactured bus passed in front of me and I attempted, like many souls before me to chase the bus along the road.

These were double-deckers probably relics from the 1930's, slow moving monsters powered by the Lucas diesel engine that made a terrifying noise blasting out clouds of toxic fumes. There were no sliding or auto doors in those days, just an opening at the rear of the vehicle where the ticket collector stood. Safety was limited to one vertical white metal pole in the opening, or footplate used to assist when alighting. For those brave enough, the objective was to run alongside the bus jump forward onto the footplate whilst grabbing the pole and hoisting one's self aboard. This I managed, which prompted a rebuke from the conductor, "silly young bugger," he remarked before continuing to issue tickets at 3p single to Manchester.

Health and safety had not been conceived at this time and such athletic activity was regarded as a badge of honour.

Not so for other suicidal maniacs who had failed to connect with said pole and landed flat on their face in the road. In those days there was little traffic, so the possibility of a fatality was rare. The only real pain was the embarrassment of walking back to the bus stop with ripped trousers and facing the more patient travellers who were less suicidal.

2. One more time

I'm on holiday and there in the distance is a bright apple red Lucas double-decker bus. Wow where did that come from? Haven't seen one of those in donkeys' years.

I'm rooted to the ground in admiration just staring at this relic from the past which now looks so magical, it's a fabulous site, it even has the original advertising posters running along the side panels. *Embassy the cigarette of choice* – you wouldn't get away with that nowadays and *Horlicks for a good night's sleep.* I wish!

It moves, slowly then gathers speed, I follow jogging, running then a full sprint, I need to catch the bus one more time. I know how to do this, aim for the white rail on the footplate and then hoist myself on board.

My imagination crumbles, as the bus heads off down the promenade, well I could do it at one time.

3. Deception - But not for long! - Manchester 1967

Having settled into a pattern of working life I am more relaxed about my travel arrangements. Lateness and the retribution that would follow, no longer hold the same fear factor. Not that I made a habit of lateness, just tried to travel smarter.

It's a ten-minute walk from home to the bus, a twenty-minute bus ride and a further ten-minute walk to the office and I'm in for 9am. So begins a little deception routine taught to me by my friend John. He and I would exit the lift at the sixth floor and head straight for the cloak room. Take off and hang up suit jacket and proceed to the drinks vending machine, where three old pence would buy a cup of what then passed as tea, commonly known as paint stripper. Stroll back to desk in main office as if we had been in for a while and just gone for refreshments. If challenged answer: "I've been here for a while boss, just getting tea".

Needless to say, that scam didn't last for long as we were rumbled, a sort of self-inflicted wound as you will find out later in the episode TV175.

There is a very strict dress code for men in the office, navy-blue suit, white shirt, (although I did flaunt that rule on many an occasion with some very bright colours) tie essential and clean black shoes. Which were often inspected by the head honcho.

By the by, on my very first day, 15th May 1966, I arrived waring a check blazer, grey trousers, open neck shirt with a cravat and brown suede shoes. Hilarious for everyone but me and they never let me forget it.

My departmental boss was a guy called Ron Hendry, very proper, punctual, always used a fountain pen - I liked that and he was a wizard at spelling. Given my handicap in that area of the English language we had an uneasy relationship for the first twelve months.

In time Ron was promoted to another office and his number two Jeff, took over. Jeff was a good guy. I went to his stag night, oh my God! the hot spots of Salford don't bear thinking about.

So, this means I also get promotion now number two and they employ a junior, Eric. I am no longer bottom of the pile, no more finger injuries from pins whilst filing, going for endless cups of tea for others, now I have my own gofer. He was a cheeky little sod, but we got on well out of work, both playing on the company football team. Also, he arrived as I was entering my Mod period which was something else we had in common. Consequently, our conversations were invariably about Motown, clothes, clubs and the advantages of the Lambretta over the Vespa.

We were in our minds 'cool' in the 60's long before this word re-entered present-day usage.

Occasionally one of the big bosses, in my case Burt Houghton, a fearsome looking ex-military man, would send for me and off I would trot to his very spacious office lined with mahogany panels and leather furnishings. There, he would present me with a cheque for 'pay bearer cash of £25', a considerable sum in those days, almost my entire nett monthly spend. Henceforth to the Williams and Glyns Bank on Oxford Road, I would go. Boy did I hold on tight to those five-pound notes on the way back, it was in some way a compliment, you felt trusted.

A normal day would begin with the post, delivered to my grey metal desk upon which I had a huge, black, bakerlite phone with a central dial. Also, a Dictaphone, same colour and connected directly to the typing pool. Post was a variety of usually twenty letters, some typed others hand written with requests from clients to change or arrange new types of insurance, ranging from Finality guarantee, goods in transit, travel, employers/public liability the lot.

These were the days before texts and emails when people corresponded with pen and ink on writing paper, enclosed in an envelope and sent by Royal Mail to the addressee. What back then took a week to arrange with letters going to and fro, would probably be done within minutes these days.

This was Area 1. General Department of the largest broker in Manchester and although I didn't appreciate it then, I was having a good time.

4. Ronnie does Elvis - Manchester 1968

Besides my department, there were others on the same floor. One specialised in fire insurance for factories and cotton mills of which there were many in the North West at that time. This was a period prior to the one-man demolition expert Fred Dibner who gained TV notoriety for blowing up cotton mill chimneys.

The main man was Ronnie Forrest. Ron was about 26 which, to us eighteen-year olds, made him almost ancient in our eyes. He played on the company football team, a well-built black-haired dynamo, position inside-left, which no longer exists in today's game. Ronnie also had a company car, a rarity back then. Your bosses provided you with a car and paid all the expenses, imagine that. It was a Ford Anglia two door, burgundy in colour and a white roof, he was the man.

Many a lunchtime six of us would pile into this four-seater on a short journey to the local chippy in Salford who did a very tasty line in chips, pie and peas.

Ronnie also did a very good impression of Elvis, full body movements and everything. Occasionally he would break into 'anit nothing but a hound dog,' or 'blue suede shoes,' just a few lines but something which would have me and Eric in stitches, this older guy doing an Elvis, hilarious!

By contrast we were into Motown, Edwin Star, all the imports from Detroit.

Next to Ronnie sat Andrew, three years older than me but it could have been ten. He had an impact on my career both whilst in Manchester and supported me when I moved abroad some years later. Andrew was clever, not just bright but he knew things other people didn't. He was one of the youngest in the country to qualify for his insurance degree, and what you might now call cool. He smoked a cigarette like Humphrey Bogart, drove a triumph spitfire, yes, a triumph spitfire! but couldn't play football for toffee. I liked Andrew and was godfather to Sam his first daughter, with hindsight something I should have taken more seriously.

On occasions, I would go round to Andrew's house in Stretford and keep him company, when Lyn, his wife was on night duty at the local hospital. A four pack of 'Long Life' lager and ten Embassy was usually enough for a few hours

Back at the office, smoking was common place in those days and ash trays rapidly filled up as the day progressed. We all contributed, from the big boss and his tipped 'Benson and Hedges', Charles Osbourne on his pipe – a major contributor - to me and Eric with our pack of five 'No 6'. By three in the afternoon the office was a potential cancer zone with a blue mist hovering over the whole room. Funny thing was no one ever mentioned the smell of tobacco on our clothes, probably because we were all bathed in nicotine and immune to the toxic aroma. This wasn't just a male preserve, females in the office contributed their share to the fog, Embassy usually their smoke of choice.

The non-smokers, poor devils were the odd ones out and no quarter was given to their need for oxygen. Passive smoking was an accepted risk, in fact 'passive smoking' wasn't even a phrase back then.

5. The All-nighter - Manchester - 1968

It's been two years since I started work and now I approach my 18th birthday.

My travel arrangements have change since my recent increase in salary, I decide the train is a better option. Plus, it's quicker and more comfortable. My annual salary has increased from the staggering figure of £365 - always remember that as same number of days in a year, ex leap years - to a mega £428pa!

After HMRC have taken their whack I am left with £30 per month. Five pounds of which goes to mum for food etc. and five buys me a monthly return ticket from Failsworth to Manchester Victoria railway station.

The remaining £20 was more than enough to cover my expenses which were mainly, weekends at the Oasis club in Manchester with Jim, Bas and Eric, when the latter decided to turn up.

Clothes were from the Army and Navy store in Piccadilly, ex-army gear was the thing to have, combat jackets and great coats - Navy and RAF were the best. These were required attire if you wanted to be taken seriously as an up and coming mod.

Just to put the cost of living into context, one could go out on a Saturday night to the Oasis club and catch the all-nighter bus back home and still have change from ten shillings. In new money that's 50p!

A point of interest: my best mate Jim met his future wife Sandra, at the Oasis when we were eighteen and proceeded to get married on Derby Day 6th November nineteen hundred and something. That night when he saw Sandra, I had never seen him move so fast across a dance floor, even when we played football he was never that quick. Anyhow he has been married now for a long time, way beyond golden and ruby it's probably called a Kryptonite wedding anniversary.

To continue. The 'all-nighter' left Piccadilly on every hour from midnight and it was usually packed. If the smoke from forty people lighting up didn't kill you then the smell of some poor soul throwing up on the back seat would definitely leave a lasting impression. When he, it was usually a he, left the bus a great cheer would break out and various versions of goodnight were exchanged between 'sickie' and the rest of us. Waving goodbye from the back window, we would wish him well and gestured that it was now two o'clock.

I digress. Back to the walk to work, which now takes in some very special parts of the city. Victoria station is a Historic building with references to the local Manchester Pals from WW1. Then on to Parsonage Gardens, past Manchester Cathedral, along the Old Shambles pub, through St Anne's Square, across King St, and finally arriving at the rear of Brazennose House, my place of work.

The return journey had its moments, I would arrive in time for the 5:30pm to Failsworth, purchase the Manchester Evening News and read about Colin Bell and MCFC. However, once the movement of the train took hold with a gentle rocking sensation, I was off to the land of nod. Sometimes missing my stop and ending up in Oldham waking with a jolt as the train came to an abrupt halt.

Taking a few seconds for reality to kick in and then racing over the platform for the train back home. Missed my dinner on many an occasion, no mobile phones to let mum know. Hence, she would worry, as mothers do.

It was about this time, February 1968 that I had a magnificent birthday present which would have yet another impact on my travel arrangements so that I was no longer reliant on public transport.

The Mod was coming of age.

6. The TV 175.

It's February 1968 and I have just been given the most magnificent birthday present.

The keys of which were handed to me by the gentlest, kind and caring man, my dad. I never got as close to him is I should have done, Ben taught me that.

There in the back yard at my home was the ultimate Mod accessory, a Lambretta TV175. White with red side panels, spare wheel and a leather seat. In time I would add six mirrors, front and rear crash bars all in chrome and a dark brown fur cover for the spare wheel. There's more; the tyres were painted white, various stickers on the wind screen and a Union Jack flies from an aerial at the rear.

I would invest in a parka with fur hood and a helmet – my blue and white skid lid - which I still have to this day.

My overcoats from the Army and Navy store of the previous year were out and in came the mod gear to compliment my TV 175, the parka.

Whilst dad and I had a good time cleaning the carburettor and changing wheels, this wonderful machine isn't the sort of thing mothers like their sons to have. Consequently, I was constantly being told to drive carefully and take my driving test. Which I did and, in the process, nearly running over the examiner.

They have this crazy part of the test called an emergency stop. The examiner sends you on a predetermined route and at some point, (it was usually a he!) he jumps out in front of the pupil and you are required to perform an emergency stop. Well he did jump out, rather late I thought, a sort of Kamikaze moment, from which we both survived.

One of my friends, who was a few years older than me - John Lillie - owned a motor bike and was recruited to give me a few lessons. We found a quiet road and he began to explain the relationship between speed, clutch and gears. Something up until then I had not considered.

I was ready, cocksure, dressed in loafers, grey slacks and my new maroon coloured Fred Perry jumper. (Emily please note, I was not wearing a skirt, but a cardigan).

I kickstarted the bike and revved the engine, remembering what my mate had said I turned the throttle and let the clutch out. Mistake....

The bike took off at a 45-degree angle and I was left in the sitting position in mid-air.

I had forgotten the word 'slowly' when letting the clutch out. The bike was fine, I however, had holes in my new Fred Perry and a huge dent in my pride. My mate on the other hand found the whole episode hilarious and dined out on this at the local chippy for weeks.

Eventually I got the hang of things and was able to synchronise the throttle and clutch to avoid any further mishaps.

No longer would I catch the bus or train to work, now I was self-sufficient and mobile. My route into Manchester was back on the road and I took delight in passing the 98 and 82 buses however, never the tankman of the No 10.

Down Oldham St, along Market St, into St Anne's Square and on to Deansgate, from where the guys in the office could hear the megaphone effect of all 175cc's bursting out of the exhaust. Which, as I found out later put paid to my usual trick. (*See previous chapter Deception*). By the time I had parked the bike in the underground car park, caught the lift to the sixth floor, found my way out of my parka, googles, helmet and gloves it was way past 9 am.

The only memorable incident I can recall was late one evening, well midnight. I had taken to turning off the engine at the top of our street and freewheeling the last 100 yards, so as not to wake the neighbours. Which was fine provided the key remained in the ignition.

On that particular night, I forgot and removed said key thereby engaging the handlebars in a locked position which left me with no control over the destination of the bike or me. In the dead of night I had announced my arrival to the whole neighbourhood.

It was a lesson learnt the hard way, god bless the blue and white skid lid. Lambretta survived for another twelve months then I changed jobs and mode of transport, enter the Hillman Imp, all 875cc.

7. The Scottish Life Assurance Company – 1970 / 74

Prior to my twentieth birthday my fashion-conscious friend John 23, moved to The Scottish Life Assurance Company in Manchester. I was still at Stenhouse Brokers and now part of the in-crowd ambling along and enjoying the comfort of a job I could do well, with no thoughts for the future.

The Scottish Life, a wealth management company, were looking for salesmen to build a network of agents across the North West. John had secured that position and was doing OK, company car, company mortgage, expenses etc. It was an incredible job with great rewards, provided you were successful. Soon he gained promotion to Birmingham office and then recommended me to the regional manager Harry Jones as his replacement. Harry was a flamboyant chartered accountant who always sported a bow-tie, a fashion item that John and I both copied – you should see my photograph, hilarious - although it didn't catch on with our colleagues. No one could wear a bowtie like Harry.

Next thing I know, I'm on a BEA flight to Edinburgh for an interview with their top man, Kenneth Bone, the agency Director. I had no idea what to expect, previous job interviews were normally a brief chat around experience, sport etc and then a job offer followed. These were the days when one could leave a position on a Friday and start a new one the following Monday. The Manchester of the 1970's was awash with jobs in Insurance. However, The Scottish Life was rather special.

Kenneth Bone's interviews took over two hours and comprised of exercises in role plays and a maths test, which I just managed to pass. All this I learned later was referred to in the company as the 'Bone Inquisition' or 'BI' as it was more commonly known.

Shell shocked after my 'BI,' I returned to Manchester and during the flight we were hit by lightning, twice! If that wasn't an omen, then I don't know what is. Glad to be back on the ground I was ready to put all that behind me and assumed they were looking for an A star candidate with GCE's in every subject including Esperanto, 'let it go' I said to myself.

You know what? I got the job. I was appointed trainee inspector for Manchester and Cheshire. Was I beginning to be influenced by the material world of company cars, company mortgages, an expense account etc? Possibly. However, I was enjoying the freedom that came with this new position, making my own plans and learning a new skill, I was looking forward to the future.

Initially, I had to complete a probationary period and learn new types of investment contracts involving Life Assurance and Pensions, note the word assurance, not insurance. One has an 'inevitable outcome the other a possibility'. That definition I had drilled into me by Kenneth and under no circumstances was I to refer to the company as anything but THE Scottish Life Assurance Company. Mention an abbreviated version such as Scot Life and imprisonment in Edinburgh Castle was assured. Not insured!

On my first day in the new job at the offices in Bridge Street Manchester I was introduced to the staff. Six secretarial support, the manager Peter Marsden and the assistant manager Jim Tetlow, one of life's real gentlemen. Then there was the dragon! There's always one, the chief clerk, Gladys in this case and they were all a little bit intimidated by her. She was pedantic in the extreme and could fly off the handle at anything that was incorrect or caused her pressure. Which, considering the business we were in, was a constant feature of the daily routine in meeting deadlines.

At least we had a one-minute warning, our own nuclear alert when she was about to explode. Her neck would change to a soft pink then slowly rising to bright red as it engulfed her cheeks and blossomed crimson on her forehead. Boom!

Out went the call, where's Peter? He was the pacifier in these circumstances and the only one able to negotiate peace between Gladys and the poor soul who had triggered her latest rant. Which was me on many an occasion, mainly due to my rather slow progress in preparing estimates and costings. Remember my maths test with Kenneth? I needed to improve and quickly.

There was one other male in the office, F.D.A.Wood, an ex-Sandhurst first Lieutenant who served in Borneo and Malaya. At 28 he was the archetypal ex-military officer, wearing the cleanest of boots - not shoes - you have ever seen, stood bolt upright as if at attention all the time and spoke with an assured crisp accent in perfect English. He was what the company called a chief Inspector, the next rung below assistant manager and about to be promoted to manager of the Nottingham branch.

One morning I was summoned to Peter's office and told of FDAW's promotion. Next, I was to be promoted to take his place! How on earth do you follow that guy? The closest I got to military service was the air training corps, at 16 and that didn't last long. A flight in a jet provost over Blackpool and any thoughts of a career in the RAF were over.

To complete my training, I had been seconded to the St Albans office for four months. This is where the hot shots of the company plied their trade, always top of the business tables year on year and it was felt I would benefit from the experience of rubbing shoulders with the likes of Mr Binder, David, John and Peter. Hertfordshire here I come.

Can't be bad I thought, four months at the company's expense in a nice hotel. Well, they had arranged my accommodation however, not what I had anticipated. I was booked into the local YMCA in Welwyn Garden City for the duration of my stay. This consisted of a bedsit twelve feet by twelve, the internal design was pre-IKEA therefore more Habitat, small but comfortable. Externally though the building resembled a disused army barracks.

Hence, this was to be my home for the next four months and over that time I would learn to live with and share breakfast and dinners with the most unlikely set of characters you could imagine. Mainly mad chemists from the pharmaceutical firm Smyth Kline and French who conducted toxic and explosive experiments in their bedsits, (the fire alarms were always going off.) Music students who were for ever playing the Russian composer Shostakovich very loud and late into the night, a full orchestral version of depressing revolutionary music. In addition, we had ex-offenders on early release from serving at Her Majesty's pleasure, a halfway house for them to practise rehabilitation on us before being released into the wider community. Not always successfully.

Breakfast consisted of cereal, nothing else was on offer. Consequently, the sanest of the bunch, a guy named Rob and I bought our own eggs and persuaded the canteen manager to make scrambled eggs each morning. Yes, we had a canteen not a restaurant and it kept strict hours, be late and miss whatever delicacy the cook had prepared that evening. Consequently, Mars Bars were a constant back up and part of my unstable diet. The other inmates of this wonderful retreat were usually to hung over in the morning to take notice of our breakfast treat, plus Rob and I were the first up and out to work each morning.

And so it was that every day I would take the bus into St Albans and arrive at Chequer St, my place of work just above the Anglia Building Society.

First to arrive was usually the chief clerk, a scot named Alex, 27, who had moved from Edinburgh with his wife and young family. I spent Sunday lunch with them on a few occasions and virtually every lunchtime with Alex in the Peahen Hotel enjoying a delicious crusty cottage pie and coke. (the drink)

Peter Edwards, 27, was the inspector and youngest, apart from me, he arrived six months earlier from Preston in Lancashire, a quiet guy I never really got to know him.

David Black, 39, was the assistant manager a short rather dour Scot, very serious and full of tradition. He invited me for Sunday lunch with his family on one occasion and appeared in a kilt!

Next, my new mentor John Kayes, 36 what a guy. I spent lots of time with John in interviews and travelling the countryside in Hertfordshire visiting members of his broker network. He always played Jimmy Young on the car radio, loved cooking and we listened intently to Jim's daily recipe, "What's on the menu today Jim?" Hilarious times.

Finally, the man himself, Desmond J Binder, 44 or as I always called him Mr Binder. He had built the business model in Hertfordshire from scratch and was a very professional, clever and fair man.

In their own way they all contributed to my training and I gained a lot of experience over such a short time. Then, a couple of days before I was due to return to Manchester, Peter Edwards was killed in a car crash. Just driving his mini to the local newsagents and then it happened.

After a couple of weeks back in Manchester Peter Marsden called me in for a meeting. Apparently, Mr Binder had asked for me to be transferred back to St Albans on a permanent basis. Peter was having none of it and I stayed in my home town for the next three years. I was no longer a trainee but a fully-fledged member of the Manchester team.

I returned to see the men and women at St Albans who helped me and attended their Christmas party each year until I left the Company in 1974.

So, there you have it, two more people who had a positive influence on my career so far, Andrew from the episode 'Ronnie Does Elvis' and the two Johns mentioned above, oh and Mr Binder of course, that's four.

Book Six - Black Dog Comes to Visit

1. The Devil Within.

Sub title. Never taken for granted

From the outside he appeared to be the epitome of the 'in-control' business man.

He strode purposely through the open door and into the building heading for the lift to the fourth floor. Gave the usual good morning greeting to the commissionaire with a flash of pearly whites that would be the envy of any Hollywood 'A' lister.

"You have to stand tall," that was the message his father had always told him, whether in a lift or on the parade ground, *"ramrod straight back."*

The lift doors open, and the highly polished black brogues take their first step onto the plush red carpet of the fourth-floor reception.

His suit was navy blue with a tooth check stripe and a single-breasted jacket. He preferred three buttons on the jacket with a pointed collar. Trousers, with pleated fronts, however no pockets. This detail was a reference to his younger days when fashion was more of an individual choice than the mass-produced styles of today's designers.

He had purposely asked his tailor not to include pockets in the trousers, he still had flashbacks of his head master at school shouting after him, *"hands out of pockets boy!"* This was the voice he remembered, the man himself, Mr Reginald Turner a fearsome retired army officer, probably put the fear of God up his troops, now drilling the young boys from Manchester.

The tie was colourful against the obligatory white shirt with cutback colour, however nothing as revolutionary as the John Snow variety.

He was fortunate that the current hair style amongst his peers was short, almost a complete shave of the head. That pleased him.

The crowning glory was the must-have watch. The heavy Omega watches, worn by his younger colleagues did not suit his slim wrists. So, he had gone for the more classic design of a Jaeger Le Coultre with original JC black strap.

Conference room one was his destination and the group were already in place when he pushed open the door. Their conversations ground to a halt as he headed to the top table. These presentations were now common place for him, he knew the script backwards, control of his tone, volume or significant pause was easy. It often seemed he was on the outside watching himself, managing eye contact to personalise a statement, making a point then slowly repeating the point for maximum effect. It was, he knew a well-rehearsed act. He regarded the content as pearls of wisdom which he had gathered from many years in the profession and in some cases, lessons learnt through bitter experience.

His assessment of the delegates after completing these talks was simple. Each generation seems to make the same mistakes in this business. Try as he may to educate them in good practice he knew they would at some point have to learn for themselves, hopefully through fewer mistakes.

It was nearing the end of today's presentation when he first noticed the change in temperature. Had the central heating been turned up? He was beginning to perspire, nothing much at first then he felt the warm beads of perspiration crawling down his cheeks.

He was conscious of his heart beating at a quicker pace and thumping louder in his chest.

To cap it all, his eyes began to water blurring his vision and that hammer in his head is now hitting the anvil hard, very hard.

This was the devil within, arriving to take revenge for all the foolhardy pleasure he had absorbed from these sort of days, when he subconsciously thought immortality was his. The suit, shoes etc. were now obsolete they weren't going to prevent this dark intruder from taking ownership of the things he had taken for granted - his physical and mental health - in which direction was this demon taking him?

Later the doctors diagnosed nothing more than a panic attack, which didn't quite fit with his confident perception of himself. None-the-less, the warning had been served it was now down to him, would he trade the suits and big boy toys for the opportunity to review his life and that of those closest to him?

He thought of his assessment of the delegates that had attended his presentations, *"each generation makes the same mistakes."*

Mistakes, would he now learn from his?

2. Smarties

"What is this life if full of care we have no time to stand and stare."

How right you are poet Bill Henry Davies.

Yet I have heard people say we humans can't mentally stand still or freeze our thoughts we are always thinking. A little dramatic, and sure in practical terms if you were to stand still in the centre lane of the M6, the train lines at Piccadilly Station or the main runway at Manchester Airport long enough you are guaranteed a result.

"But it's not that kind of standing still, it's up here".

He points to his head.

I've heard him preach like this for years and never really connected. I knew he was on medication, a real cocktail of drugs that had changed and increased over the years that it was now a way of life, or, not to put too fine a point on it, maintaining an existence. No one professional had ever monitored his situation, in fact the only time that happened was when we had private medical insurance and would see 'Dr A' whom I christened 'Dr do little' for reasons which will become all too apparent shortly.

Every two weeks we would visit his private rooms and wait in the Victorian styled reception hall for our turn. After registering our arrival with the 'lifeless' receptionist, one could then avail one's self of the hospitality offered by the clinic. This extended to a coffee machine - brew unknown - Country Life Magazines and easy chairs for clients and their bewildered relatives or friends who accompanied them. The place was adorned with lilies, expect nothing less at Dr A's prices. The 'lifeless' one would call out a patient's name, rather indiscreet I thought, and so began the climb up the zig zag wooden stair case to Dr A's consulting rooms on the first floor.

Dr A recommended changing meds with great frequency, when one didn't work, then try another. It was like handing out smarties, if the blue one isn't suitable then let's try red or yellow. Never mind the after effects of coming off one and the side effects of the new magic bullet. This is what he did and always after consulting his pharmaceutical guide book kept in the top right-hand draw of his mahogany desk.

I often thought it would be less expensive to buy a copy of that manual and decide for ourselves on which one to choose next.

Eventually we became what one patient referred to as 'financially cured', humorous yet deadly accurate. Roughly translated this meant the insurance company had decided enough was enough and they withdrew cover at the first opportunity.

What next then?

Dr A suddenly became unavailable, no social, medical or professional responsibility. You were on your own and without that magic book from his top draw.

Answer, back to the NHS.

If you were lucky then you had a GP who retained a basic understanding of 'the illness'. Unfortunately, they were ill equipped to do more than put you on a different smarty.

Referrals to NHS specialists were like 'hens teeth'. One had to wait months and then it was a trainee who wanted to hear your life story. Sometimes they suggested keeping notes of mood behaviour and record these highly personal details on a photocopy of a photocopy, weekly page diary. How would you rate your mood that day on a scale of 1 to 10? *"Well Sherlock let's start with a 0 and go from there"*! Was what I felt like shouting.

I always regarded this as demeaning, however any port in a storm, and I realised the trainee was just going through the prescribed motions, so they could record another 'case study' for their tutor.

That was all a few years back. Since then I succumbed, I didn't take Bill's advice, I didn't *'stop and stare'*, or the modern equivalent which is, "smell the roses or coffee."

I did the opposite of standing still, my brain went into overdrive, work was all consuming. Going to sleep and waking up with those destructive thoughts, to me it was natural, I could cope. This was working at speed, 110mph in the fast lane and I was in control. Well, life has a way of putting an end to that sort of arrogance and so it did. Mentally I went from 110 mph to a standstill, I didn't see it coming. Just like a car accident, my brain went through a windscreen, only this wasn't a physical windscreen it was the mental equivalent of a crash.

Consequently, I find myself trying to reduce my meds down from 3.75mg to 1.85mg and hopefully zero. Small doses you might say, however let's take a look at these little smarties, white in colour and tiny. Size has nothing to do with it, neither, depending on the individual, does the strength. Once inside your bloodstream, then they are off on a journey that takes them into the brain, unknown territory, like Scott in the arctic and we know what happened there. These little white smarties are, I am told supposed to build bridges to ensure receptors are connected and working properly. Well that's fine I'm sure the pharmaceutical companies have done the required amount of research and clinical trials to satisfy the appropriate government bodies. If you are lucky and they work for you, then stay on them. By the way have you read the list of possible side effects on the slip of paper that accompanies each box? If that warning applied to any other food or product you just wouldn't buy it! The lawyers obviously earned their fee with that disclaimer.

If, like me you decide to come off the little smarties then this is where the fun starts and you need to check again on the withdrawal side effects of your intended journey into masochism. Additional details on google. *Other search engines are available.* Once you have acquainted yourself with this rather distressing information and you decide to continue, then good for you and God help you.

What I wonder would have happened, had I put aside days to get off the merry-go-round of life and taken my mind for a rest.

Who would make that decision, certainly not the me of 30 years ago. But now, would it be the older me typing these letters or the kinder young boy who first occupied this soul.

Is he still there asking to be relieved of his pain?

3. Thoughts of an unknown – 1920

Taken from the book: Gniddik Tsuj
(note: The T is silent)
By the Norwegian Author: Ewol Knarf. 1895 – 1937.
(note: The K is silent as in Knutsford)

Looking out at this view of the Mediterranean one would either have to be from another planet or ill at ease with oneself, not to appreciate the beauty of this place.

Come with me for a while and observe my world. We'll start with the 'feel good factor' on a scale of one to ten, the latter (ten) being Euphoric, I rate as a two.

Yes, it's a beautiful view, quiet, peaceful and a wonderful cornucopia of colour. The sea and the sky meet as one in glorious electric blue. The lemon trees in full fruit, the yellow and green should promote a feeling of wellbeing, an inner peace. However, if the fragile brain receptors are inactive, then nothing happens, just a thick fog occupies the mind and thoughts choke before they can escape.

Looking around at my fellow diners I wonder where they are on the 'feel good scale'. How many traumas, disappointments, haunt their thoughts right now or have left a scar that surfaces from the deep recesses of memory, particularly at that deathly early morning hour of three o'clock before sunrise.

Are they trying to be happy and show the world everything is ok, genuinely on another plain where the beauty of this place has a positive influence on the soul? Or does the heavy weight of pain lay abandoned in their throat allowing the sadness to linger, beckoning black dog to come calling.

How long ago was the damage done that resulted in this sadness, maybe a bad experience as a child, stored yet long forgotten, or a bereavement that was never mourned?

If the body can develop a cancer then why not the soul? What mental hurt was inflicted on the child, too young to understand the infection that was taking hold, through no fault of their own, but introduced by adults, their guardians?

No external beauty will cure this pain, only the arrival of sleep offers a limited respite. The damage has already been done by previous generations and there is no mindful penicillin that can heal his fractured soul.

Like millions he suffers alone only the demons past and present to keep him company.

Book Seven - Odds & Sods

1. Rorke's Drift. 22nd January 1879

It all started with Rorke's Drift, you know the film with Michael Cane and Stanley Baker.

This was the rather harmless discussion I embarked upon with my son and heir one Sunday evening in early August 2017. Ben was using the formation adopted by the Zulus as a template for the MCFC attack this coming season. What MCFC were going to do to the opposition was, well frankly bordering on illegal and painful for any defender.

Back to the conversation, of course it wasn't right to invade the Zululand in the first place, but this was and to some extent has been the way of most industrialised nations who look to expand their empires.

Rorke's Drift was a side show given the bigger conflict that was going on in Africa at that time between the Boers and the British. We Brits weren't the only ones taking advantage of the situation in Africa.

Several European countries were at it from the 'Belgians in the Congo' (Billy Jowell, he of, 'we didn't start the fire' and Vincent Kompany). To the peace-loving Portuguese - birth place of Vasco da Gama and the 'special one' - in Angola, let alone the Germans of course.

By the way the Red Coats were outnumbered slightly, not sure of the actual figures but 3000 v 175. You would expect the home team to win, no not in this case it was an honourable draw, thanks to Michael and Stanley for Oscar winning performances. With eleven Victoria crosses awarded to the away team.

Back to the discussion, which by this time was gathering pace at a rate of knots. Me, talking of the historic references of exploitation, land grab and general greed of so called civilised nations. Just look at Britain for example, we've been invaded by the Danes and Romans even before Bill from Normandy decide to have a go in 1066.

Also, further afield in Europe they have been at it for thousands of years, the Egyptians, Greeks and again those pesky Romans conquering half of Europe and Asia Minor. Let's not forget the Spanish and their atrocities in South America. The Incas were happily carrying out their ritual killings as sacrifices to their gods at the Machu Picchu temple, until the conquistador found they had gold in them their hills!

Finally, there was a little French guy who had ambitions above his station and wanted to conquer GB, Spain and Russia. He was given the Elba and ended up all alone on an island.

No, not finally, there's more. I start on the Brits; disenfranchising the Aborigines in Australia and the US who systematically removed the indigenous Red Indians to 'reservations.' In the process George Armstrong Custer and his mates sending a lot of them to the final happy hunting ground in the sky. All that after their own Civil war!

Ben, by now is blazing a trail with a narrative about narrow minded people with ill-conceived and badly informed ideas. Mainly 'Daily Mail' readers, who apparently cannot think for themselves.

None of the above events are excusable, however, to quote Edmund Burke, '*the only thing necessary for the triumph of evil is for good men to do nothing.*' History is a great teacher if only men, yes men would learn the lessons from history and more women were in influential positions, then the world might be a better place.

Boudicca - pronounced the old way - was cut off in her prime by the Romans and Joan of Arce didn't make it beyond the age of 19, appearing painfully as the main attraction in a bonfire.

So, will Angela and Teresa make a positive contribution to world peace, will the French president's wife guide her pupil and will Ivanka become the next and first woman president of the USA?

2. Boots.

Now, as Moi said, "You might think a boot is just a boot, but it isn't," and certainly not when I am the buyer. I have a knack of making the simplest of tasks agonisingly difficult and frustrating for those around me. (Also see chapter on Llandudno by the sho-er.')

On finding a classic shoe/boot advertised in the GQ magazine, I embarked on a mission to find and purchase a pair. My search in Manchester proved surprisingly unsuccessful and so I turn to the manufacturers web site, no less a maker than Crockett and Jones, boot makers of repute in Northampton since 1878.

There, on the screen in front of me is the classic Coniston boot in dark brown leather, six different photos projecting their elegance and style. The very name radiates a sense of history, craftsmanship, wellbeing and quality. Apparently, they are made on a 325 last, the significance of which I know not. Although, I understand it has something to do with width of shoe and importantly how long the leather is retained on said last. *Google for more info, other search engines are available!*

Also visible are the distinctive four eyes for lacing and six top clips to secure the laces.

The excitement gathers a pace as I see my 'soon to be' boots are available from the C&J branch, Colmore Row Birmingham, a size nine and a half, perfect.

A quick phone call to the assistant Dan H secures the items, an obscene amount of money is paid by my flexible friend Mr Halifax and said Boots are winging their way to Burnt Acre. Oh, joy of joys.

They arrive, strip back the paper and there is the famous C&J box with gold lettering. Inside are the beautiful dark brown leather boots, wrapped individually in their green cotton boot socks.

I take my time to appreciate the craftsmanship and potent rich smell of fresh leather before trying them on, after all this has been a successful search for a quality and much sort after item; one has to savour the moment. Grasping the necessary shoehorn, I slide into the boot, well there's the problem I didn't just slide, my foot fell into them, they are too big! Try as I may to convince myself otherwise it's no good my feet slide back and forwards inside the glorious leather.

Following several minutes of disappointment, tinged with a fair amount of panic, we, rather Moi suggests I contact the supplier and check for a size nine. What a good idea, which I follow to the letter. However, Dan H at C&J does not have this size in stock, all branches are sold out. Apparently, they only made a minimum number as a trial and it has been very popular.

Can I order a pair? "Yes," confirms Dan H, however they are six weeks on the last - there's that 'last' again and with Christmas approaching it will be well into January 2018 before they are available. After several more attempts at trying to convince myself they fit perfectly and much deliberation I return boots size nine and a half to Dan H, and await refund.

We fast-forward two weeks when I visited my local town and given I was near to the shoe shop, I called in. Surprise, surprise there on the display shelf is the Coniston. Problem, it's in bright tan and they only have an eight and a half, which is just a little too tight.

You still with me because this is crucial? By process of elimination the shop owner and his assistants, yes I have everyone involved in the next big decision, we go for a size nine in dark brown. They place the order and yes I am prepared for the six weeks waiting time.

It's now the 10th January and the anticipation grows daily, I begin to wonder are my feet still the same size, have they swollen and will the new size fit? Paranoia sets in.

To be continued.

3. If's its good enough for Neil Armstrong......

'Thump' that's the postman delivering today's unnecessary advertising leaflets and more trees gone!

Considering the drop from the letter box to floor is less than four inches my curiosity is awakened, what would cause that noise from such a shallow drop?

The answer was contained in one of those 'jiffy bags,' very secure but a devil to open. After several attempts with scissors and a kitchen knife to gain access, I found inside, a device that was available to me, 'as a special customer,' and at a very competitive price. I discard the now blood-stained jiffy bag and read on. This is the latest in hearing aids or as the advertisement boasted, 'It will help you rediscover the voices of your youth.' Not so sure that's what I want to hear again.

That's not all, get this, the device had been tested during the NASA moon landings, well I suppose if its good enough for Neil Armstrong then its good enough for me.

Now I had been accustomed to receiving leaflets, personalized letters and free consultations, however nothing compared to this free trial of the actual item. The accompanying letter was, I thought, rather amusing as it referred to the free trial and I quote as it appeared in bold lettering;

A REVOLUTIONARY HEARING AID!

A tad over the top as there was nothing wrong with my eyesight. Basically, this was a sixty-day free trial, just plug it in and off you go, no fuss on returns.

However, I had my reservations considering all the problems I had experienced with another device called 'Alexa'. You know the one I mean, you talk to her and she is supposed to find answers to everything. Well lately she had developed a mind of her own, making unilateral decisions on what she thought we wanted. Just turning on at random and giving the weather forecast in Beijing without warning. I was becoming a little suspicious, was this another listening device introduced by

Amazon or another international business, seeking world domination in the supply of goods? Would they be listening in on my inner most thoughts, measuring my buying signs with access to my brain from this 'hearing aid?'

Possibly even a Russian plot to control the minds of the materialistic westerners?

Paranoia had set in.

I had to concede my hearing was not as sensitive as it once was. There were times when members of my family – yes you know who you are – would often shout, "Are you going deaf?" when I failed to catch their every word in conversation. Further episodes followed as with my neighbour who tried to strike up a conversation with me on football. He said, "Well done City, they are a real hit of a team."

Unfortunately, I miss heard and thought he had employed another letter in front of hit, to which I had taken offence and replied, "Your lot didn't do any better," which left my neighbour confused yet thankfully not offended.

On other occasions I had been completely oblivious to conversations and just replied, "yes," or "sure," not knowing what I had agreed to or with. So, now I am very conscious of this irritating piece of plastic nestling in my ear and I begin to talk louder to hear myself speak, which is both ludicrous and counterproductive.

Also, those who notice the device when talking to me, speak slowly applying great attention to their pronunciation and very loud. I even attracted attention from a couple who tried sign language with me. That didn't go well. I thought they were the ones who were hard of hearing and attempted my own version of hand signs.

I'm not sure what message I gave out as they took one look at each other and retreated quickly into a crowd for safety.

By this time, I have convinced myself I needed the device and before you know it, the sixty days of the trial have gone by and the ninety-five pounds monthly payment has kicked in. I must have missed that small print. Maybe I do need an appointment with the opticians!

4. Llandudno by the shoe-or

How many times would you return a pair of shoes if they were the wrong size?

Once? Maybe twice? Surely not three times? OK four, yes four, that's me or rather Moi and all in the space of an afternoon.

What does it take? Charm, courage and sheer bloody mindedness.

We were on the Welsh Riviera, Llandudno to be precise, not everyone's cup of tea, however for some reason I have a need to visit this seaside town once a year.

Whilst reading the latest GQ magazine I noticed Rob Lowe (no relation) advertising Skechers shoes and thought I could get away with wearing those, add a pair of designer jeans take off thirty-eight years in age and that's me.

Coincidentally, there is a local stockist of Skechers and within half an hour I was in there enquiring about said shoe, size nine and a half. Problem, they don't do half sizes. Now get ready, there are a lot of numbers in the next few paragraphs so keep up.

So, it's either a 9 or a 10. We go for 9 on the basis I will not be wearing socks. Back in the hotel room straight on with the Shoe. Something is wrong, they don't feel right, should have gone for the 10. So, Moi goes back and returns with the 10.

No, not right, my feet feel lost in these cavernous shoes. So, rather sheepishly I ask Moi if she would mind returning and exchanging for size 9, definitely 9. You still with me? Good.

You are probably wondering, why always Moi who goes back? Well they know her by now, that's my excuse plus the reasons in paragraph three above. Yet within ten minutes of returning to our hotel we agree they are too small, and it must be the 10. Final answer yes final answer and to prove my decision is final I discard the now dog-eared receipt to the rubbish bin.

By now Moi is almost best friends with the sales assistant and luckily, they see the funny side of the afternoon's events. So, it is with relief I open the box and find the size 10.

On reflection this was about to become my worst hour, I can hardly bring myself to say the words which we all know are coming! As I scramble for the receipt which is by now doing its best to avoid me, settling in a darkest corner of the waste bin. I coax it out and we decide this is the last chance, in any event the shop is about to close in ten minutes.

Moi leaves the shop with the size 9 and is sure she saw the assistant race to lock the door and immediately engaged the closed sign where upon the assistant and cleaner ran for cover behind the shoe racks.

5. Flu and Enza come to call

One of the earliest references to influenza is from the Greek physician Hippocrates (460-370BC) whom the Hippocratic Oath is named after.

There are various theories on the origin of influenza, one of which refers to a mythical Greek yogurt farmer called Nicholls de Fluenza. It was around 500BC and Nic the Greek had two daughters both of whom were mischievous throughout their early life, chasing the goats away so the yogurt production fell below EU quotas and making un-lady like gestures at the Japanese tourists.

Things got so bad for Nic' and his five sons that he banished the girls from the family home, casting a curse that they should grow old and live forever.

It back fired.

On hearing this news both daughters vowed to roam the earth bringing discomfort and pain to the male species. The elder of the two Flu, now 23 and her sister Enza rampaged throughout the centuries and were the cause of the black death plague of 1348 and great flu pandemic of 1918/19.

Flu and Enza, still abound to this day and search out the unsuspecting male of the human species to inflict the most uncomfortable and misunderstood illness known to human kind, namely Manflu!

By the way their first victims were their father and five brothers. Boots the chemist was still thousands of years away. Consequently, they had to rely on goats milk, honey and a generous shot of ouzo to see them through a painful few months.

Manflu differs from other strains of influenza in so much as it is neither tolerated nor understood by the female of the species. Complaints of a sore throat that feel like it has been scrubbed with a wire brush, sinuses that ache with every sneeze and the constant flow of various unsightly liquids from the bright red nostrils are brushed aside.

So, what does the average male do?

Either. Makes an effort, showers, dresses and gets ready to leave for work, with the mother-in-law of all headaches. Drenched with perspiration and a temperature of 101, he is met by Mrs who states, *"what are you doing up you look dreadful, you should be in bed!"*

Or. Decides to take a day off work, keep the infection to himself and stay in bed, at which point he is told, *"you don't know suffering, you should try giving birth, that's pain."*

You can't win, not that it's a competition, but you just can't.

I'm off to bed.

6. Do fish need water?

I'm having a conversation with myself at the moment and talking to me about the things we have seen today for our next story which I will now share with you…"

Today I throw off the safety harness and puncture the cushions of my comfort zone in the coffee shop of choice and look for alternative places for inspiration.

Inspiration to write the next chapter in the book that by now, I should have circulated to several publishers, however what have I done? Answer, *Didley squat!

Possible definition: Didley Squat (DS) was the son of Jeremiah Hamish Squat, who emigrated from Glasgow to America in the 1750's and Little Pink Feather – whom he married in 1770 - daughter of chief Running Water of the Powhatan Indians.

On reaching his eighteenth birthday, their offspring Didley, joined the American Navy. His service record describes him as lazy and prone to catnapping whilst on night watch. His shipmates, who by this time were fed up with his idleness, decided to teach him a lesson and one day threw him overboard.

*The story gained traction and his name became a by-word for **inactivity or laziness**.*

*By the way, he managed to swim ashore and there he remained, re-registering his rights of ownership to the piece of land now known as New York. **Note**, this may also be the origin of the term, 'Squatters Rights,' however it is yet to be confirmed*

Apart from a lame attempt to speak with a publisher on LinkedIn, which has probably found its way to his spam box or he engaged the ignore button, I have done DS.

Oh, and not forgetting the publishers in London who closed their doors and portals to 'New manuscripts'. I linger on the word **manuscripts, what a fabulous sounding word, full of maturity, honesty and antiquity.

**Taken from sixteenth century Latin 'Manuscriptus,' meaning 'manu' (by hand) and 'scriptus' (written.)

It would seem the world and his wife have taken to writing books so they (the publishers) are swamped with would be J.K Rowlings.

If, (such a small word but what power of consequence it holds), yes **if** you do find one that is open for manuscripts then be prepared, the criteria for submitting your life's work is as follows:

Electronic submissions Only

Cover letter in email

A short biography

Synopsis

Flexible file formats accepted (.doc .pdf etc)

email subject: Book Submission -

Name your attachment(s)

author title of book

Full Manuscript

This may not seem a lot to some people however, after slaving over your creation you are now faced with what I call the 'Aintree factor' at work. So many hurdles, then once you think you have navigated your way over and through the obstacles, you must do it all over again for a second time. However, should you be a footballer – usually retired – celeb or have appeared on the One Show then no problem, nepotism is alive and thriving, skip numbers 1 to 9, go straight to publisher and print.

***Sour grapes?

Correct.

***Sour grapes is a term applied to someone who could not take defeat gracefully or envious at another's success, which he/she felt they should have enjoyed.

Possibly originated from the Turin Wine Festival of 1903. Alphonso (Al) a French vintner from the Champagne Valley was most upset after the judges awarded the Premier Rosset to Leonardo from Ravello. They [the judges] concluded the wine produced by Al was sour, a verdict he took badly. Which became known as the Sour of Al's Grapes. Eventually shortened to sour grapes.

So, where has my out of comfort zone experiment taken me today? It's the Hanging Dog pub come restaurant and I arrive at 3.30pm with the place empty, the lunch trade having gone, yet leaving samples of what satisfied their hunger lurking on the carpets. Empty that is except for Trevor (Trev) who has been here since noon and is as ****'Happy as Larry'.*

*** *Origin: Believed to be Laurence 'Larry' Foley, an undefeated champion Australian boxer during the 19th century. In 1879 the street fighter turned professional boxer, reportedly won the Australian championship in bare knuckle boxing bout. A New Zealand newspaper apparently ran a story about the win which described the crowds as being as 'happy as Larry.'*

Trevor is one of those *"everyone is my friend"* imbibers with an ear to ear grin stretching across his cherry red face. This is partly covered by an enviable mop of black hair that hasn't seen a comb since Jesus turned water into wine, his head rocking like those miniature dogs in the back of a driver's car.

Here is a word of warning, which you ignore at your peril. Should you find yourself in a similar situation, standing next to a 'Trevor' at the bar, then do not make eye contact with him otherwise you are destined to be his next best friend.

I made that mistake and for the next half an hour I and the barman are cornered by Trev spouting forth on the problems of global warming, the price of beer and the self-centred egotestical politicians, his pronunciation now severely hampered by the beer. On Brexit, he hardly stops for breath and takes no notice of my interjections preferring to laugh at his own jokes instead. Put him in a room with Barnier and Co and I truly believe we would have a deal within the hour.

*****"One for the road"*? asks the barman of Trev.

"Do fish need water?" is the reply from my new friend.

****Origin. *Various, however the one I like best is that it derives from the supposed practice of offering condemned felons a final drink or two at pubs on the way to the place of public execution in London - The Tyburn Tree. 16th through to 18th centuries.*

This is my time to leave the premises and I exit with Trevor serenading me to the door, in what he believes to be his best impersonation of Frank Sinatra. He leads with, "*Oi, my mate, where are you goin?*"

Then begins to sing, "*it's one for my mate and one more for the road.*"

Ps. It was after this day's events that I met Lionel. Yes, you know who you are. He listened and gave me a chance, so take heart not all publishers are the same.

7. "I thought you a said PSI test?"

I recently attended hospital for my annual blood tests, all the usual ones, cholesterol, prostate and many others.

At my GPs request I was now waiting my turn at the surgery to hear the results. Apart from the little fellow throwing Lego around the room and the piped musica, all was peace and quiet. Anyone with a minor headache was now sure to be on their way to a full migraine as pieces of Lego bounced off the walls and Bruce Springsteen blasting out from the radio with, 'Born in the USA'.

Eyeing the suggestion box I can't resist and pen a short note stating, "given the reasons people are here it might be a good idea to choose a radio station which offers music of a more peaceful nature. Hard rock is not conducive to patient's state of mind, also ban Lego!"

Having deposited my written protest in the box, I head towards the magazine table only to find back copies of 'The complete Angler', 'Hare and Hounds' and the usual dog-eared 'Hello' magazines.

For alternative entertainment I could watch the TV screen anchored to the surgery wall, now showing, 'How to avoid a cold', 'Government recommended units of alcohol,' and 'Watch for the signs of Chlamydia.'

It further goes on to state that abuse of staff will not be tolerated. That's fair enough but what about the music abuse from Little Mix and Buoyance that are now pounding in my ears?

Additional entertainment can be found in the numerous pamphlets pinned to the notice board on self-help groups, *if you've got it, they can help*. Well, when I say *they* I mean *you* the volunteer. However, you will need to attend a six-week induction course and endure endless PBS checks. Now there's an idea for another self-help group for volunteers who want to volunteer but find the process stressful. But there's already one for stress.

Patients come and go as I continue to wait, friends are reunited when they notice a familiar face entering the surgery and the usual questions are asked, "Hello Mary how are you"?

"Fine," she answers with a smile.

What the hell are you doing here then!? Is what I feel like asking.

They then go into a huddle and it's at this point I assume the real reason for her attendance is revealed. A couple of "ooo's," sympathetic "ar's," and the alarming, "oh dear," spring from members of the group.

At last my name appears on the TV screen with, 'GO TO ROOM 4.'

This should be straight forward I've known Dr Alice for years and it's only a review. She runs through the various results which mean little to me and then states the PSA test was fine however adding, "We normally combine this with a manual examination, just to be sure".

"I thought you said it was a PSI test?"

"No Frank I'm not testing your car tyres more your prostate. So, as you are here let's do that now."

I don't think so! Next, I hear a voice, it's my mother asking "Have you clean underwear on?"

"Yes" I say out loud in answer to my mother's question.

"Ok let's get started," replies Alice. Then I realise she thinks I have agreed to, well you know, the procedure.

I could never look Alice in the face again after that examination, never mind when we next meet and her last image of me, doesn't bear thinking about.

"Is Peter in?" I ask, praying for a celestial intervention.

"Yes, I can ask him if you prefer," said a relieved Alice.

Poor Dr Peter he gets all the man-type afflictions to deal with.

In he strolls, no hellos straight to the point and instructs, "step behind the surgical white curtain please and get ready." I know what he means and do as I am told, then I hear the all too familiar slap of a pair of Gladys gloves being prepared.

Curtain drawn and from the other side one probably has a rather bizarre view of two silhouettes in action, well one at least.

Had this been a movie then the censors would have slapped an X certificate rating based on the following couple of scenes.

Job done and I am passed back to Alice, "take a seat she offers".

Are you kidding, after that, I'd rather stand.

Pete and Alice have a quick chat and then he's off to accost some other poor fellow.

Book Eight - Poems & Plays

An Alternative outcome

1. Charge of the light brigade
(as experienced from an equine point of view)
(With apologies to Alfred Lord Tennyson).

Its October 1854 and the British Cavalry are in the Crimea near Balaclava.

"Half a league, half a league, half a league onward. All in the valley of death rode the six hundred".

Wow, hold on there, cowboy...what's all this, *"valley of death business?"*

If you think I am going down there, *'Cannon to right of them, Cannon to left of them, Cannon in front of them,'* you are very much mistaken, my friend.

In fact, if you are so keen, then I invite this great heavy lump on my back to dismount and you gallop down the valley yourself matey. That sort of commitment is way above my hay grade.

Anyway, who wrote this poem? Alfred Lord Tennyson? Is he a Lord?, and if he's that committed, then let him get down on all fours and accompany you towards those Russian guns.

Yes, I know he didn't give the order to charge and is only providing us with a very dramatic narrative of that fateful day. However, maybe we could employ a little artistic licence on the result of that action, less blood and guts, more life and glory"?

Too late, I can see through the fog they are all coming back, well maybe not all, 195 of them. 405 didn't make it and we could have been the 406th...

What a cock up between Raglan, Cardigan and Nolan. Those three are on the transfer list for next season.

Brave fearless boys Alfred.

Foot note: Yes, peerage in 1883.

2. The green eye of the little yellow god.

A poem believed to be written by either J. Milton Hayes 1884 – 1940. Or Rudyard Kipling. 1865-1936.

"There's a one-eyed yellow idol to the north of Kathmandu. There's a little marble cross below the town".

"Not anymore," shouted the man from the highways department, his high viz jacket blowing in the breeze.

"What do you mean? It's in the poem, ask John Milton Hayes, he wrote it."

"I thought Kipling was the author"?

"Never mind that, they've put a road bypass in and moved the idol. Health and safety got involved."

"And the little marble cross below the town?"

"Gone too."

"So, it should read."

"There's a one-eyed yellow idol to the north of the M62?"

"Yes".

"There's a little marble cross next to McDonalds, off Junction 6?"

"Yes".

That's ridiculous, it's supposed to be in Kathmandu!

Correct however, following discussions with the Home office and the Indian High Commission we moved the location to Bradford in Yorkshire.

But Kathmandu is in the Federal Democratic Republic of Nepal.

Why did you do that?

Well there aren't many Nepalese in the UK, however, there is a large Indian community in Bradford and it's more relevant and up to date, more socially inclusive you might say.

Apart from the Nepalese you mean?

What about: *"There's a broken-hearted woman tends the grave of mad Carew?"*

Can't say 'mad' anymore, *psychologically challenged* might be acceptable to the censors.

"While the yellow god forever gazes down?" Go on tell me, you're not happy with that either?

No, you can't use colour and a religious higher being in the same sentence that's blaspheming. So, it's, *"and the multi-racial higher being forever gazes down."* Is that acceptable?

Yes.

Let's recap, see if I can get my head around this. Your version is going to read:

"There's a one eyed multi-racial higher being to the north of the M62.

There's a little marble cross next to McDonalds off Junction 6.

There's a broken-hearted woman tends the grave of psychologically challenged Carew.

While the Multi-racial higher being forever gazes down."

As a matter of interest just when are you intending to transfer this sacred shrine to Yorkshire?

All done mate, opens next Monday.

What do you mean opens?

Entrance fees are £6 for adults, half price for OAPs and £3 for children. McDonalds are giving double fries to anyone who shows their entrance ticket to the shrine.

Didn't the Nepalese object to this monstrous act of vandalism?

No, we gave them the Millennium Dome and Wayne Rooney in return. Coleen seemed quite pleased.

.

3. Save the Boy - Casabianca (1826)

A poem by Felicia Dorothea Hemans (1793 – 1835)
Cast:
Boy on the burning deck, Casabianca: Himself
Felicia Hemans: Herself
First man on the shore the observer: you the reader
Second man on the shore, Louie: Louie Wash

"The boy stood on the burning deck. Whence all but he had fled"
"Hey Casabianca" shouted the man on the shore, *"what are you hanging around for, that ship is well on fire?"*
"This is what Felicia wrote so I have to follow the script" He replied, looking rather flushed.
The man intervened.
"Felicia can you please do a quick re write this kid is only thirteen and will expire shortly if he stays in your poem for much longer"
"You ask me now after all this time, its 2019 and I wrote the poem in 1826" she exclaimed. *"Let me get my quill"* and *I'll see what I can arrange."*
"Forget the quill lady, use the key board on the lap top its quicker"
"Lap top, key board what on earth are you talking about man"? "I've run out of ink, so it will be a while, the maid has gone into town for me and will not be back before sundown."
"But it's only ten in the morning" shouted the now very impatient observer. *"What's she doing walking"?*
"Well how else is she supposed to travel on those country lanes"?
"Forget the maid just use your mobile and phone Amazon, what are you on Virgin or EE"?
"Now you're just being offensive and rude, I don't know any EE and as for questioning my virginity that's going too far"
"Madam" shouted an exasperated observer, *"you might as well be living in the nineteenth century, send a text instead then.*
"I am and what has sex got to do with it"?
"Not sex I said TEXT"!

"I have no idea what you are talking about and anyway how did you manage to contact me"?
"I Googled you"
The man's obscene, thought Felicia.

"I'll dictate a better ending if you use your, whatever it's called."
"Take this down" ordered Felicia.
She continued. *"The boy was on X factor and stood upon the stage, Simon Cowell and panel thought he was all the rage."*
"And so he won the competition, acclaimed by all to reign, however, like all winners before him never to be seen again."
"How's that"? Asked Felicia
"I'm not sure about the never to be seen again bit however, provided he goes on to make records and survives that's fine". Sighed the man.
Then a new voice from the shore shouted *"I have a better idea, set the lyrics to a rap version and I'll form a boy band"* claimed an eager Louie.
"No thanks" replied Casabianca, *"I'll take my chances in the rest of the poem."* And with that he dived into the sea and swam ashore.

4. About Harry - Two sides of the same coin.
Based on the poem 'Leisure' by William Henry Davies 1911.
"What is this life if full of care we have no time to stand and stare"

"Druggie, zombie, drunk, get a job," are the accusations I hear thrown by those staring at the haunted souls I see standing motionless against the wall. These unfortunate zombies – *that's wrong, he's a human being and deserves respect, a name so I call him Harry* - is so high on the latest drug it prevents movement. They crouch like human black bin-bags, in a doorway, near a cash point or just leaning against the wall outside Manchester Piccadilly Station. It is there that two things pass him by, time and commuters, fellow inhabitants of this tiny planet.

What's his story, how did he reach this point, craving to avoid the waking hours and longing for whatever lies on the other side of that chemical high. Who provided this cocktail that offers mental freedom from the rigours of the conscious world? For a while I try to make sense of this, however, I hit a mental brick wall, then count my blessings that, like many others I have been spared the events that took Harry on his journey searching for an escape.

The comparison with the other group who 'stand and stare' couldn't be more visible. These are the celebrity football spotters who spend most of their Fridays and Saturdays routed to the pavement outside a coffee shop in a Cheshire market town. Cameras at the ready they wait patiently, waking only when the blast of an exhaust introduces the arrival of the latest Ferrari or Bugatti.

And so, we are introduced to a different life, a few miles away on the outskirts of the city there is another tortured soul. However, his life, as seen by others is different. Instead of walking-by, people wait for him to appear, drive miles just for the chance of a photograph. They have time, they make time for their hero, they don't see him as a druggie or drunk.

Sure-enough the roar of an exhaust is the fan-fair that precedes the canary-yellow Ferrari. Cameras click, necks are strained as the group capture their latest photograph of the car and the driver, instantly posted on Facebook or whatever is the latest form of, *"I'm here look at me,"* social media communication.

What a contrast between Harry and the driver of this canary car, who believed he had 'made it' with all the trophies of success on display, the car, house, friends (*he will find out soon enough if they are real or just hanging on*) and the bank balance. That's the perception from the outside.

Maybe the driver is living with his fears locked away from public view behind his own 'Mexican Wall' built of Temazepam and his new-found friend Johnny Walker.

In the early hours of the morning he finally succumbs to sleep, and it is then that the *night frights* begin, he lays there unable to move, zombie like. The savage wolves form a circle and his wakening cannot come too soon for him.

In contrast, Harry, sits motionless against a glass door, head bowed, seemingly in a comma and possibly dreaming of that Ferrari, the good life and this is where he wants to stay. Simultaneously, as the driver regains consciousness and strains for oxygen, followed by a sigh of relief on ascending into his world, Harry awakes and so begins his decent into *day frights*, his world.

Harry just stands and stares, his wolves are gathering and will remain with him until he can afford the next exit pill.

So, *"what is this life if no one cares, how long will you let Harry continue to stand and stare"*?

5. Macbeth (The Scottish Play) by Willian Shakespeare. 1606

Location: On the high street near Greggs bakery, Glasgow town centre.

Police sergeant Mackey approaches the three millennials.

They are chanting, *"When shall we three meet again?"*

"At the next WI meeting, salsa class in Handforth maybe, or Zumba next Friday night?" Asked Mackey

They continued, *"In thunder, lightning or in rain?"*

"Why always in bad weather, why don't you girls go out on a sunny day?" Continued Mackey.

"When the hurly burley's done, When the battles lost and won." They cried.

"You'll catch your death of cold dressed like that tonight, split jeans, long black capes and pointed hats anyone would think it's Halloween. Och, hang on, its only 1606 and Halloween hasn't yet been transported back from the colonies. The latest fashion it may be, but you look weird and young ladies should be off home before the pubs close, what would your parents say? Assuming these little feral sisters have any," sighed the Searg.'

"I hear Macbeth, Banquo and Malcolm are out on the lash tonight. You don't want to be around when those three are on the razzle. Complaints for harassment will ensue and I might have to throw them in the stocks for the night. That Maca is one nasty piece of work, he's gone off the rails since he met that woman, mark my words there's a 'tragedy' in the making."

"His Missus, Lady Macbeth is off seeing her sister in Aberdeen, so they decided to have a boy's night out. There'll be hell to pay if she hears of this, seeing daggers and all that hallucinating about being Queen of Scotland she's really got visions beyond her station that one."

"All right sergeant Mackey, we'll away to our coven," and off they went singing a little ditty. *"Double, double toil and trouble fire burn and cauldron bubble."*

"*That will never catch on,*" thought Mackey. "*They need to rap it. What am I thinking, your too old for this man. I'm away to my *boushty before Macca hits the streets.*"

*Boushty. An Old Scottish term for bed.

6. The Owl and the Pussycat by Edward Lear – 1871

The cast: Eddie played by himself Mr E Lear
Prompter: Mr. T Toad
The interrupter: You the reader

The Owl and the Pussy-cat went to sea
In a beautiful pea-green boat,
They took some honey, and plenty of money,
Wrapped up in a five-pound note.
The Owl looked up to the stars above,
And sang to a small guitar.

"*That's impossible,*" *shouted the man in the front row of the theatre.*

"*So, let me get this right Eddie, a bird and a cat, not usually the best of friends, set off in a boat, colour pea green, to get married. Is that even legal? Well yes maybe these days but not back in 1871.*"

"*Also, the Owl just happens to be a classical guitarist, and can sing. Come on!*"

"*Later in your poem, they meet a pig who sells them a ring, which was until that time secured through its nose and are then married by the vicar who is a Turkey, and finally have mice for their wedding supper? Which I suppose is rather a natural meal for birds and cats however, not very sociable given the occasion.* "

"*Did anyone attend the ceremony, apart from the Turkey and Mice who didn't stay for long. Were there any other witnesses? Next, I suppose you will tell me they had children?*"

"*Yes, is the answer, later in the sequel, they go on to have a child although sadly the pussycat dies when she realises, too late, she can't fly like her mate the owl and plummets from the tree. Thereby dashing the claim that cats have nine lives,*" Replied Eddie

Having had enough of these interventions Eddie signalled to the usher at the rear, "*Please show this gentleman out.*"

"*Certainly Mr Lear,*" replied the big brown bear. And with that another disbelieving human, void of any imagination was ejected from the theatre on to the streets. Much, I might add to the amusement of the chickens and fox in the rear stalls.

"*Now where was I* "asked Eddie

"*And sang to a small guitar,*" replied Mr Toad the prompter.

"*Thank you, Terry.*"

7. From Through the looking glass 1871 by Lewis Carol

The cast:
The constant interrupter: you the reader.
Lou: Mr. Lewis Carol playing himself

The time has come,' the Walrus said,
To talk of many things:
Of shoes — and ships — and sealing-wax —
Of cabbages — and kings —
And why the sea is boiling hot —
And whether pigs have wings."

"Hold on, since when do they speak English or any other language?" asked the interrupter.

"How do you know they don't?" replied Lou.

"Well it's a well-known fact, that apart from humans, other inhabitants of this planet can't speak."

"But they do communicate with one another in different ways and are very intelligent. For all you know that parrot over there could be a professor in parroting and the frog in that long grass may have a PhD in pond life. Furthermore, see that swallow, the way he glides through the air, he could be an aeronautical engineer or a pilot."

"No, sorry Lou I just don't get that and another thing, later in the poem, you introduced these trusting oysters who were lulled into a false sense of security by your two scheming main characters. They walked for a mile along the sandy shore, tired them out, then they ate the lot! That's not a very Christian act is it? "

"I haven't finished yet, before we go any further, how come a carpenter meets up with a walrus?"

"If you must know it was through a dating agency on the dark net". Replied Lou.

"Wow something for everyone these days, do you have the email address?"

"No, be off with you, otherwise I will write you into this poem and marry you off to a pig."

"OK keep your hair on Lou, you always did live in a wonderland."

And with those fateful words the interrupter married the porkie!

8. The Scarlet Pimpernel.

By Baroness Emma Orczy 1905.

'Robespierre and a bad day at the office'

They seek him here,
they seek him there,
those Frenchies seek him everywhere.
Is he in heaven or is he in hell?
That damned elusive Pimpernel.

Maximilien François Marie Isidore de Robespierre, to give him his full name had a problem. The revolution was going well, 1789 had been a good year however, the headcount had been dropping in recent months.

All, he believed due to this 'pimpernel' character and worse it was thought he might be an Englishman who was helping the French royals, bourgeoisie and professional classes to escape from France and avoid the chop. The English, he mused, nothing but a nation of shopkeepers.

Robbie, as he is now known to us, was vexed. He called in his assistant, citizen Louis.

"Citizen I have a task for you. We need to employ a Frenchman to find this pimpernel. Who is the most famous detective in France, Maigret, Inspector Lobel or what about that eccentric little Belgium Poirot, he would do?" suggested Robbie.

"Citizen Deputy, they are all fictional characters of the future, the films haven't been made yet," Replied Louis.

"Then who else"? demanded Robbie

"What about Napoleon, he is a second lieutenant in the French Artillery. However, he will eventually become the most famous French man ever," was Louis's reply.

"Where is he?"

"He's sulking in Corsica."

"*Then employ someone to find him and bring him back here,*" instructed Robbie

"*Your losing your head,*" whispered Louis under his breath.

"*What was that,*" barked Robbie?

"*I said take it as red.*" And with that he made a quick exit to execute his task.

A week later Louis returned to meet with Robbie for his CPD and performance review.

"*Well, has your detective found Napoleon?*" asked Robbie

"*I'm afraid not citizen Deputy, he's quite elusive,*" was Louis's defence.

"*I'm intrigued, tell me more about this detective you employed?*" enquired Robbie

"*One can only contact him through a third party and he's a very private person you know. He is, as I might have mentioned an Englishman and has rather an amusing nick name of 'pimp'.*" Louis Laughed. "*Apparently this is due to the fact he introduces young ladies to the English aristocracy.*"

"*So, Louis, you sent someone you have never met on an important mission to find Napoleon and this person, did you tell him the reason why we wanted Napoleon?*"

"*Of course, citizen*" replied Louis.

"*Tell me Louis, does that description of this Englishman with the amusing nickname remind you of anyone else?*"

"*Well now you mention it,*" started Louis who was beginning to go rather pale. He was not allowed to finish his answer.

"*Well indeed, sounds very much to me like you employed the person we most want to capture, to find the very person we need to capture him*".

"*Tell me Louis have you met madam G?*" asked Robbie.

"*No,*" sighed Louis.

"*Then I must introduce you,*" replied Robbie sporting a broad grin.

The last thing citizen Louis saw from his uncomfortable crouched position was the old ladies knitting and then a sharp pain in the back of his neck.

"*Next.*"

9. Romeo, Juliet and Roger.

Taken from: Romeo & Juliet by William [Bill] Shakespeare - cerca'1590. Performance: Act 2 Scene 2.

Actors: Juliet Capulet and Romeo Montague.

Location: A Balcony in the house of Lord Capulet [Juliet's Father] overlooking the Orchard.

Venue: Verona, Italy in the 1300's.

"O Romeo, Romeo, wherefore art thou Romeo"?

This is the opening sentence of a romantically philosophic speech by the character Juliet. Its literal meaning is that Juliet is agonized to think that Romeo is a Montague, and painfully wishes him to have been from some other tribe (family).

What she's really saying is, *"Where the hell have you been man? I've stood here for the past two hours spouting these lines and you go missing. Well?"*

"Hi Jules, been down the crucible snooker hall with cousin Benvolio and Mercutio, the World championships are on and Ronnie's playing."

"You get yourself up here now and finish this scene, my feet are killing me, and I need a drink. You spend too much time down that hall watching O'Sullivan, no wonder you can't be on time for rehearsals and as for your lines, can you remember what comes next?"

He mutters to himself, *"Shall I hear more, or shall I speak at this?"*

The play dictates that Juliet shall have the next five minutes of the play to herself, she continues,

"Tis but thy name that is my enemy: Thou art thyself, though not a Montague," etc. etc.

So, relieved Romeo takes a break to check in with Benvolio and reaches for his Vodaphone. *"Hey Benni, it's me. How's Ronnie doing? Break of 120 you say, that's good I'll be over again as soon as I can."*

In answer to Benvolio's question he continues, *"She's still harping on about this and that, boy can she talk, it's a nightmare. Can you imagine what she'll be like when the football season starts? We'll be lucky to get to home matches let alone a day out to Napoli for the away game."*

"It's different when the tennis is on the box, put Nadel, Federer or Djokovic on and she's frozen to the box. I shouldn't complain, however, Wimbledon is once a year whereas our season is thirty-nine weeks and that's not counting the cup final."

"Hold on, she's finished early," exclaimed Romeo.

Juliet finishes with, *"Romeo, doff thy name, and for that name, which is no part of thee."*

After a long silence and no help from the prompter, Juliet throws the script down to Romeo and follows up with, *"Here get it right for once, you tosser."*

Romeo, *"Ta Jules, Henceforth, I never will be Romeo".*

"Cut, cut," comes the voice from the side of the stage. *"Romeo, in the words of Lord Sugar, you're fired,"* shouts Bill the director.

"Someone find me the understudy, we are recasting and changing the title "When Juliet met Roger, can't be any worse"!

"Want to bet!!"

10. Maca and Maca go into pantomime.
(With acknowledgement to William Shakespeare)

'Lead on Macduff' is an invitation for someone to take the lead and that you will follow on. But as any keen Shakespearian scholar will tell you, this is a misquotation from Shakespeare's Macbeth, Act 5, Scene 8.

The phrase should be *'lay on'* which means to make a vigorous attack. The words are spoken by Macbeth to Macduff. They are in battle and Macduff challenges Macbeth to yield. Macbeth refuses, declaring:

> *I will not yield,*
> *To kiss the ground before young Malcolm's feet,*
> *And to be baited with the rabble's curse.*
> *Though Birnam wood be come to Dunsinane,*
> *And thou opposed, being of no woman born,*
> *Yet I will try the last. Before my body*
> *I throw my warlike shield. Lay on, Macduff,*

"Come on Macca don't be so dramatic, it's only a commercial for incontinent pads," replied Macduff.

"Tas come to this that I, who was destined to be the next King of Scotland should have to prostitute my talents in this way," moaned Maca.

"Look we have to pay next month's rent, and this is a nice little earner, also now that Ant and Dec are no longer an item, we could be the next presenters of 'I'm a Celebrity, Get me out if Here,' if we play our cards right," replied Macduff.

Macca had fallen on hard times since he failed in his attempt to complete a takeover of the Kingdom. His wife had gone nuts, hallucinating about seeing daggers and he was on the run for arranging the murder of his best friend Banquo. So, disguised as Maid Marian he was doing commercials with his mate Macduff.

The only thing they had lined up was a ten-week Christmas pantomime of Robin Hood and Maid Marian in Llandudno. The offer was too good to turn down particularly as Maca was masquerading as a woman. Unfortunately, the part of Robin had gone to Ed Balls, consequently, he was not looking forward to the more intimate scenes. Poor Macduff was lumbered with playing Friar Tuck.

Came the beginning of rehearsals for the panto and Maca was dreading the thought of wearing women's clothes for the next ten weeks. He was a wanted man; his picture was all over News at Ten and this make-up was playing havoc with his skin.

None of his mates could call him as the police had tabs on their phones. Even worse, he was acquiring an unwanted reputation in the local pub. He kept walking into the gents, in the dress, when out for a pint with Macduff.

The panto finished after Christmas and for the most part Maca had managed to navigate his way around Ed, hence no embarrassing moments, like facial stubble meeting facial stubble.

In fact, their performances were so good they were both invited on to 'Big Brother,' at which on entering The House, Macca was heard to say, *"Lead on Macduff."*

Wrong!!!

11. From Paris to MCFC via Barcelona

Location and Time: The Court of Louis X111 King of France.
Somewhere in the suburbs of Paris, France. One summers evening
8.00pm GMT in 1628.

Players: Athos, Porthos, Aramis and D'Artagnan (known as
D'art). Cardinal Richelieu (the villain) Chief Minister of State to
Louis.

Team: Paris St German (PSG)

Dropping his boots and kit on the table outside the 'Cloggers
Arms,' Aramis turned to his team mates. *"We'll stop and have a*
pie and a pint here."

"Don't you mean a baguette and a glass of wine?" replied Porthos,
continuing, *"We're not in England yet, however with the right agent*
we soon will be, and there, we will play for the maestro."

Aramis replied. "Get used to the local brew, although I believe Aldi
do a very nice line in Prosecco."

Whilst waiting for their mixed order the three boys had a 'kick
about' on the green facing the 'Cloggers.'

Meanwhile a coach and horses pulled up outside the pub and
it was at this point Athos miss kicked the ball, which shot in the
direction of the coach. As the young traveller alighted the ball
caught D'Artagnan (D'art) full in the face leaving the *ADDIS*
trade mark firmly imprinted on his forehead.

The three collapsed in laughter, shouting, *"Hey boy, return the*
ball."

"You, yes you, the fat one," shouted D'art, *"I demand an apology*
for this injury and insult."

"On your bike sonny Jim," replied the fat one.

With that D'art slapped Porthos across the face with his
football shorts and demanded satisfaction by way of a duel. The
matter was to be decided in the traditional manner, by way of a
game of soccer, where D'art insisted he taking on all three.

And so it was, the size of the pitch was agreed, coats were placed at each end to represent the goals and the 'offending' ADDIS football was placed on the centre spot. Being a team of one, D'art was allowed the kick off, which in hindsight was a mistake for he dazzled the three with Cruyff turns, Ronaldo step-overs and the Best, in dribbling skills. Within in a few minutes it was three nil to D'art.

All good things come to an end and so it was with D'art, who didn't see the tackle coming his way from the fat one. The first he knew of this was the hard landing on his derriere, much to the hilarity of the three defenders.

"What was that," complained D'art.

"That," said Athos, *"Was a little movement I learned from Vinnie Jones."* He then offered his hand to D'art and the four called it game over. They exchanged stories about how, as children they wanted to be the King's Musketeers. Then, after watching Pele' on French TV, deciding football was their goal.

D'art had travelled from Gascony hoping, like them, for a trial with the great French team PSG.

Over the next few weeks they each had a successful trial with PSG and the manager, Cardinal Richelieu, offered each of them a place in his team, who were about to take on the mighty Real Madrid in the European Cup final. This competition excluded the UK who had exited the tournament following a massive victory over the French at Agincourt in 1415 and decided to go it alone. (Thereafter known as the Brexiteers FC.)

PSG went on to win the final, which was attended by many of the leading football coaches of their time. The Kaiser from Bayern Munich, De-Vince of Juventus, Zoro from Real Madrid, William Wallace of Stretford Rangers and a young guy called McCartney from Liverpool.

The Cardinal wanted to sign all four on long term contracts, however, there were lucrative offers from the other clubs watching the game. In the end the four turned down all offers stating it wasn't about the money.

"Well there's a first," said the Kaiser.

Porthos began, *"It's the passion, beauty of the game, the sky-blue shirt against a lush green pitch and the fans."* And with that they all declared, *"Its one for all and all for Pep!"*

Paris to Kings Cross station was an easy journey through the Euro tunnel. However, the journey from London to Manchester was a tad more difficult, there being no motorways in England until the mid-1960's. So, an overnight stage coach with a change of horses at Watford Gap was the quickest route.

See below: A selfie of the four in their home made Blue MCFC shirts taken on a bridge over the Manchester Ship Canal near Deansgate.

Unperturbed, on reaching Manchester our four adventurers began their search for the stadium, only to learn that MCFC would not be formed until 1894 and it was now 1628. Also Peps great, great, etc, etc, grandfather hadn't been born yet.

"What was all that in Paris then, just a figment of our imagination?" asked Athos.

"Yeah, it's your fault, you up there with the pen. We never had these problems when Dumas was writing our scripts." With that they all began to tear bits of writing paper and ink off this page and threw them at the writer of their story. Exhausted they sat down on the Moss at the side of the Maine Road and began to sulk, (in French)

OK, said the writer let me see what I can do. There is a small fishing village East of these lands in Spain called Barcelona, they are looking for new young players and from what I hear they are quite good.

"OK," said Aramis *"and if that doesn't work out, I'll start a new business selling men's aftershave".*

However, that's not how this story ends. The rivalry between the amigos was so intense that D'art replied, *"It has to be named D'Artagnan Cologne!"*

"Nonsense," replied Athos. *"Athos for Men; that will appeal to the guys out there."*

"Impossible," shouted Porthos. *"It needs to multi-task, Porthos beard moisturiser."*

Ok guys, we will have to settle this in the time-honoured fashion, with a duel."

So began the longest game of football ever recorded, a four-way competition with the first to score 5,000 goals declared the winner.

The kick off was held on the 1st of July 1629, under a clear blue sky. Over time, as each of the original four collapsed on the pitch their next of kin came off the bench and took on the task. The rules - agreed on that day in July - allowed for a daily six-hour rest period, which of course they all had to take at the same time.

Then, finally in 1968 the representative from the Aramis family scored the magic goal to reach 5,000. That clinched the game and the Aramis range of men's products was launched which made millions.

That's not the end of the matter.

No.

Each of the losing families filed a law suit against the Aramis family, you see [they] the Aramis family never patented the formula of the aftershave nor registered their rights to the Aramis name as a marketing logo. Also, the original score sheets, on parchment, had deteriorated over the centuries, consequently there was a dispute on the number of goals each player had scored.

After appealing to a variety of magistrates at the highest level and getting nowhere they took the matter to Supreme Court, Judge K Mayberry at the European Court of Justice.

By now its 2019 and on the night before the verdict was to be delivered the last surviving member of the Aramis family, Aramis X1111 [14th], went to bed early. He fell into a deep sleep and had a vivid dream, a bit like Martin Luther, not the Irish guy, the other one, the African American preacher.

He, along with the original four friends were sat in the top tier of a football stadium, it was midnight and a magnificent blue moon filled the clear skies.

Aramis turned to number 14 and said, *"we have finally arrived East of the Land we first came to all those centuries ago."*

With that they unfolded a banner that draped over the top three tiers of the hundred thousand-seater stadium. From his position Aramis the 14th tried to read the banner, however, all he could make out were the letters, E.R.A.H.S.

On waking, next morning Aramis knew what he had to do, he recalled the phrase that had been passed down over the years *one for all and all for one.* His ancestor and his mates were individually brilliant, however, as Aristotle observed in 360BC, 'the whole is greater than the sum of the parts,' they were a team.

His decision, to share.

Note: *Acknowledgement. Based on the 'Three Musketeers' written 1844 approx.' by Alexandre Dumas père who was born in Villers-Cotterêts, France, on July 24, 1802.*

Book Nine - Playing with History

1. Henry V111ᵗʰ (28 June 1491 – 28 January 1547)

Location: *Hampton Court London.*

The phone rings, ringtone from Tina Turner, *Simply the Best.*

"It's Pope Clement the seventh from Rome for you sire," said Eric the Kings PA.

"Hi chlamydia, how you doin?" asked Henry.

"Henry please, its Clement as you well know and as you ask, I am a little perturbed. I hear you want to break away from Rome and start a new Church of England. This, I assume is because I won't sanction your divorce from Catherine of Aragon, so you, can pick up with that floosy Anne Boleyn."

"Yes, that's correct. I will exercise my 'divine right as king' and Brexit from Rome and the rest of you Europeans. I don't need a referendum for that. What I do want is an heir to the throne which is something Cathy can't provide me with."

"Hair, what do you want a wig for," said the slightly hard of hearing Pope.

"No not hair, I need an heir to the throne who will reign after me," said an exasperated H.

"Its fine here no sign of rain," came the reply from the deaf one.

"Mad cleric," thought Henry.

"Listen Clemi, I'm off to sort things out, speak later."

"I need to get the ball rolling on this, send for my chancellor," instructed Henry.

"You don't have one sire, no one wants the job after what happened to Wolsey, Moore and Cromwell," replied Eric.

"What"! Exclaimed the King

"Can I speak candidly my lord, without fear of retribution?" asked Eric.

"Get on with it, man," encouraged H.

"You have acquired a certain reputation and developed a clinical approach in dispensing with three chancellors, not to mention the fate that awaits Anne Boleyn and Catherine Howard."

"How do you know that?" asked H.

"I have read the history books and seen Shakespeare's play my lord, it's not good for morale when people lose their heads. In court they talk openly and refer to your actions of decapo."

"I thought they were ordering more decaf coffee."

"No sire, it's their abbreviation for decapitation, when you assist another unfortunate soul to meet their maker."

Eric continued. *"You're paranoid man, you should chill out, you have a chateau in Boulogne, well you own the city, castles galore in Wales and a fleet of fifty ships in which to take a cruise."*

"The Spanish Armada is not due until 1588 when your daughter Elizabeth will instruct Drake to sort them out, so relax."

"You're not getting any younger and you will never fit into that suit of armour that you bought from TK Max again. You might as well send it to the charity shop. Look at your picture, you eat for ten men and look like …."

"OK Eric don't push it, anymore or there'll be more decap."

Henry thought to himself, maybe I should quit while I'm ahead or at least whilst I still have mine.

2. Title: Caesar out for a stroll.
From Julius Caesar: by William Shakespeare

Time: GMT 8pm on the 15th March 44BC
Location: Ancient Rome outside the Theatre Pompey.

Caesar smiled to himself as he took in the evening air. The ides of March had nearly passed, and he was still alive which made a mockery of the prediction voiced earlier by the soothsayer Spurinna.

It was a warm evening and he decided to take a stroll to the Theatre Pompey and catch up with his mates on the latest signings in Serie A, including Ronaldo's recent transfer from Madrid to Juventus.

Passing Spurinna on his way to the Theatre he teased her, smiling and saying, *"The ides of march are come."*

She, replied, *"Aye, Caesar; but not gone."*

'Creepy,' he thought and quickly moved on along the cobbled streets, his sandals flapping as he walked. *"I must take these to Timpsons for repair. I can't wait until Scholl invent the memory cushion inner sole and those Skechers are to die for."* Which was, in hindsight, a rather unfortunate comment.

There was a small crowd congregating at the entrance to the theatre and he recognised Albinus, Cassius and Brutus amongst the group.

Caesar greeted his friends – friends, that's a laugh – in the usual Roman way, *"Quod suus 'guys' fieri?* or the non-Latin version, *"what's happening guys?"* They in turn acknowledged his presence, forming a close circle around him. This is very friendly he thought only to find the guys had a surprise waiting for him. Knowing it was Caesar's birthday soon *(13th July)* they had brought along a gift, it was a pugio *(short Roman sword)*. Each one of his friends were keen to force their gift on him.

Who would be the first? It was Cascar. *"Here you go my Emperor, have this."*

Game over and Brutus turned to the rest of the assassins, *"Everyone back to my place for dinner,"* at which Caesar's last words were.

"Et tu Brute," or *"I ate too Brute," referring to the fact he had a prawn sandwich earlier.*

3. No Parking Ticket!

The scene: *Adapted from the play Richard 111 by William (Bill) Shakespeare. circa 1593. Act 5. Scene 4.*

Period: The Wars of the Roses England 1455 to 1485

Protagonists: Henry (Tudor) Red rose of Lancaster and (Dickie) King Richard 111 (Plantagenet) White rose of York. (Stan) Lord Stanley, Earl of Derby. Henry's stepfather. With (Al) Albert the innocent peasant.

Location: A country lane near Bosworth Field Leicestershire 22nd August 1485 (Battle of Bosworth, the final battle)

....

Albert was on his way to Bosworth, a journey he made every Wednesday morning. Normally it's a quiet ride to market astride his faithful old Mule Dobbin. However, this particular morning he was aware of a commotion on the top field, men shouting, fireworks were going off and he could see the tops of banners waving in the breeze.

'Another one of those rock festivals,' he thought to himself. *'Noisy buggers, always around this time of year and they make such a mess when it's all over, just like a battlefield.'*

Up ahead he saw a figure coming towards him dressed in what looked like medieval armour. *'It's not a rock concert but one of those battlefield re-enactments and this character has lost his way.'* He mused.

As the figure came closer, Al could see the man was stooping like he had a hunched back. Fully clad in armour from neck to toe he really looked the part.

"*So, who are you supposed to be then, Richard the third I suppose?*" asked Al with a smile on his face.

The blooded figure looked up at Al, "*Got it in one,*" replied Dickie. He continued, "*A Horse, a Horse, my Kingdom for a Horse.*"

"*Very good, just like Bill Shakespeare had written it, or will do in a hundred years' time,*" replied Al. "*However, you would be better off getting the number 32 bus from down the road or call yourself an uber cab.*"

The man persevered with his request for a horse, explaining how he had a bust up with his cousin Henry and needed to get as far away as possible. So, Al made him an offer of Dobbin for this so-called Kingdom, in the full knowledge that he wouldn't get far and anyway his mates would probably pick hm up and Al would retrieve Dobbin.

And so, it was that Dickie, astride old Dobbin rode off, or rather strolled off down the lane. To signify ownership of this 'Kingdom', Al was given a gold ring - probably from a Christmas Cracker he thought – with a strange symbol on the front.

Not long after Al heard the sound of galloping horses. He turned to see several other re-enactors dressed in similar garb astride these fine beasts which came to a halt inches from his face, their heavy breathing forming clouds around his head in the cold morning air.

"Have you seen a man on foot walking this road of late?" asked the big guy on horseback.

"Might have, might not," quipped Al, thinking there was an earner in this if he played his cards right.

The big guy lifted the visor on his helmet, "Stan, attend to this man," he barked.

'Not such a bad day after all,' thought Al, with what he was about to be paid for information he could probably buy a horse, Dobbin was history.

Al felt the cold steel of the knife against his throat.

"Now you little tosser answer Henry or ...."

Before Stan could finish Al blurted out his meeting with Dickie and pointed to where he had strolled off on Dobbin.

Stan remounted his horse and was about to ride of in pursuit when Henry noticed the sun reflecting off something on Albert's third finger left hand, later to be the title of a record by Diana Ross and the Supremes. With that he dismounted and approached Al.

"Where didst thou acquire this?" asked Henry pointing to the ring on Al's finger.

Al was wondering, what a strange way they have of speaking, and was about to ask why, when he remembered the cold steel, best not.

"Tis mine sire," he answered. *"Now **I'm** doing medieval speak,"* he thought to himself.

"So, cousin Dickie you have disguised yourself as a lowly peasant, yet your ring giveth you away as the King of England."

The outcome changed the lives of both men.

Firstly, as much as Al tried to explain he could not convince the knights of his innocence. He was press ganged into playing the part of Richard 111 and became a member of the (REC) Re-enactment Entertainment Company. Amazingly, he went on to become quite a celebrity and over the next twenty years collected two BAFTAS an OSCAR and appeared on the One Show, twice.

For his part he only had one line to remember,

"A Horse, A Horse, my Kingdom for A Horse".

As for the real Dickie, he and Dobbin lived to a ripe old age. After Dobbin passed away at ninety-two, Dickie quickly followed his old pal. The story doesn't end there for in September 2012, during an architectural dig his remains were discovered buried under what was now a city council car park in Leicester. The parking ticket remains unpaid.

Then on the 26th March 2015 the remains were reinterred at Leicester Cathedral as the real Richard 111.

Had he and Al not met on that Autumn morning who knows how that might have changed the course of history?

4. Windsor Weekend Leisure Breaks

(Henry Vth by William Shakespeare circa 1599)
Location: Agincourt, (Azincourt) Northern France.
Date: 25th October 1415.
Home team: 36,000 including men-at-arms, knights, crossbow men, the lot.
Away team: 9,000 including 4,000 archers.
Henry (H) King of England addresses his troops as follows:

We few, we happy few, we band of brothers
For he to-day that sheds his blood with me
Shall be my brother

"You serious your majesty?" came the question from the archer in the front row. He continued, *"about being your brother?"*

"Metaphorically speaking," replied Henry.

"Never mind the meta' what's it, if we get stuck into those Frenchies today and get a result then we are brothers, that's what you said"

"Well yes," replied H.

"Ok Henry, so me and the missus can come and do a stopover at Windsor next weekend, seeing as we are family, an all"

"Way I man, me to," echoed the Geordie. *"Me and the lads are away to the final at Wembley, that's not too far from Windsor and we need a bed for us and the bairns that night."*

Others started to follow suit with requests for accommodation and dinner or special rates for breakfast from the local MacDonald's.

"Hold on," pleaded Henry. *"This is not a Travelodge it's my ancestral home and anyway there's not enough room."*

"Not according to google." Came the response from the techie in the group. *"There are 1,000 rooms and it occupies 13 acres of land, plenty of room for all your brothers and their families. We can pitch tents and have a barbie' on the lawns make a weekend of it."*

"All hail brother Henry," came the cry from his new relatives to be.

"OK, OK we'll sort the Frenchies out then arrange the accommodation afterwards," said Henry. Who, by this time had realised the error of his speech and the fact he had just increased the number of places for Christmas dinner by 9,000 plus their families, less casualties from today's event. Cook would not be pleased.

Bryn, one of the Welsh Archers saw an opportunity here and was busy putting together a brochure on package tours and weekend breaks at Windsor for his friends back in the valleys. Marketing the leisure breaks would be easy now he had the royal crest of his 'brother' Henry, however, he needed a brand name. Air2B he thought, no that will never catch on, what about Home with Henry or HwH, that would sell.

*"Just before we all get carried away with this extended family, what's all this - **sheds his blood –** business?"* asked one of the more inquisitive members of the group.

"Well you can't just sit here and shout insults at them, throw a few sticks and stones and hope they'll go away. You will have to engage with the enemy," replied H.

"I'm not getting engaged to any Frenchman," cried Taff. *"I've a wife and twelve kids back home in Rhyl".*

"No, no, no, you ignorant lot, I mean you will have to make contact, beat the living crap out of them and in the process you might, only might, sustain a few bruises, the odd broken finger nail or, lose a couple of limbs," replied H.

Moving on quickly he continued. *"It's getting late so here's what we do, you lot stand over there and when I say go, fire your arrows at the oncoming French cavalry, they'll get stuck in the muddy fields then we'll all go over and get a few souvenirs, OK?"*

And that's roughly what happened.

Unfortunately for the excited archers their holiday plans to stay with their new relatives at Windsor never materialised. Henry stayed on in France and died of dysentery some seven years later. All that camembert and frogs' legs, very bad for the English digestive system.

By that time a young French girl named Joan [1413-1431] was making a nuisance of herself, constantly giving the English a bloody nose whenever the two armies met.

She was eventually captured and became the star attraction at a bonfire celebration held in her honour by the English.

John Palmer *alias* Richard (Dick) Turpin Esq. (21.09.1705 – 07.04.1739).

Occupation: Horse Thief and Highwayman

Location and time: A deserted spot somewhere on the London Road to York early morning.

With an acknowledgement and apologies to the Victorian novelist William Harrison Ainsworth.

The words every coach driver in the eighteenth century did not want to hear pierced the foggy morning air. *"Stand and deliver!"*

Basil pulled hard on the reins to bring his team of six to a halt, with the thought, *'not again'* running through his mind.

The two greys and four black horses came to a stop, their nostrils firing clouds of warm air into the atmosphere, they too were probably thinking the same, in a horsey sort of way.

Basil was the driver on this overnight express from London Euston to York Minster and filling in for a colleague who had called in sick with cystitis.

This was the fourth time in a month he had been stopped and people were beginning to question what was wrong with Basil, is he jinxed or, well you can guess, his employers were suspicious. He had started working for the Virgin Coach Company six months ago directly after qualifying as a Coachman Driver. Until four weeks back he had a perfect record and was on course for 'Coachie of the year' award. Then it happened, he ran into or was held up by Richard and he knew what was coming next.

Richard sat astride Black Bess, pistol in hand, *"everyone out,"* he ordered. Then one by one the three passengers emerged, alighting the coach and standing side by side on the muddy London Road in the cold night air.

"*Well who do we have here?*" exclaimed Richard. "*Messrs Cameron, Osbourne and Barnier and where might you be heading?*" he asked, pushing the barrel of his pistol into Ozzies nose. Feeling somewhat threatened Ozzie informed Richard they were on their way to meet a Ms Sturgeon from bonny Scotland, with a plan.

"*Treacherous dogs are you looking to topple Mother Terresa*"?

Then came a voice from on high, it was Basil. "*You've got no room to talk,*" he exclaimed. "*You ride in the dead of night, hold up innocent people with your one-shot pistol, which is probably a replica from Toys R Us and you talk of treachery. I've had enough of this young Dickie.*"

With that he climbed down from the coach and began to lecture the four on their moral conduct quoting, the philosophers Aristotle, Plato, Simon Cowell and Mary Berry. When he had finished, he took Richard on one side, "*Look Dickie, I know you from when you were a kid and knee high to a grass hopper. I used to go to the match with you and your Dad.*"

"You're not very good at this highwayman lark are you, for one thing your mask keeps slipping and I recognise your voice, so, tell me, how did you know about to-nights run and the other three times?"

Richard felt guilty, *"OK sorry uncle Basil, it was the guy who went sick, he works for me, his initials are JC."*

"Jesus Christ!" shouted Basil,

"No not that JC although this one does think he is at times"

"You mean Jeremy Corbyn?"

"No, Clarkson, Jeremy Clarkson, the presenter from the TV series Top Coach."

The outcome was thus:

Cameron, Ozzie and Michel were relieved of their jewellery and Euros. Richard then sent them off down London Rd back towards Euston, minus their britches.

Hence the Act of Union with Scotland, which had only been enacted in 1707 was maintained and an early divorce from our relatives on the continent is delayed for another 279 years.

As for Dick, the last anyone heard from him was via a Christmas card sent to his mates at the Thieves Nest Pub in Essex. This arrived twelve months to the day after he was hanged at Friergate, York on 7th April 1739 on a charge of horse theft. Ironically, the coach carrying the mail was hijacked and letters were only discovered months later following the capture of the highwayman - allegedly the Rt Rev Dr Bishop Philip Twysden (*1713-1752*) - at which point they [the letters] were sent on to the addressees.

About Basil, he emigrated to America, some say with a fortune in jewellery and started up his own coach service, which he called 'Wells Fargo'.

Book Ten - Jamaica 1974

1. #Hashish tag - High at the Hyatt

It started out as an innocent invitation from two Dutch friends for drinks. You know the sort of thing, *"come over to our place this evening."*

So, we (Moi and I) did.

Their place is an apartment at the Hyatt Regency Hotel in Ocho Rios, Jamaica. It was 1974 and I had secured a position with a firm of Lloyds Brokers.

"How the hell did you manage that?"

"You might well ask." Well that's a story for another time, but now I was being paid to do a job in paradise!

We are on the sixth floor of the most prestigious hotel on the North Coast and looking out from the balcony on a view of Turtle Beach a cappuccino shade of brown and Dunn's River Falls, where you can hear the water cascading down from the mountains to the beach. Its eight ish and the sky and sea melt together like treacle and custard to form a laser blue background.

The cruise ships have now departed taking with them their sun-baked cargo of tourists, armed to the hilt with their holiday souvenirs, which never seem to have the same allure when you get them home. They will probably end up as gifts to relatives and friends.

The views, the friends, the dollars! It can't get any better, well I'm told it did. I'll explain:

"What would you like to drink," asked our host. So, I'm thinking when in France its wine, Russia Vodka at home in England Beer. Hence why not try the local brew, again. [It] 'Appleton' Golden Rum near 40% proof with measures a tad more generous than those served at the 'Builders Arms' at home. This stuff was liquid gold and would knock your socks off if you were wearing any. It was inexpensive and wonderful with coke, ice and lime.

However, with everything there is a price to pay and this rocket fuel was guaranteed to inflict gout after three month's exposure. Known locally as the ex-pats ruin and I was no exception, one needed a course of antibiotics and vitamin B shots to rectify any joint and liver damage.

The B, as I recall was administered by Nurse Hortense Nelson via her syringe directly into one's rear parts. *"Just drop your shorts a lickle bit Mr Frank,"* then whack it was like throwing a dart, straight in the muscle. Ouch!

To continue:

"Smoke," what an attentive host. That sounds good as the hotel have the big brands, *"Dunhill, B&H or even Rothmans,"* I ask?

"No," replied our host, repeating slowly this time so as to ensure I got the message, *"Would you like a smoke?"*

Ah, the penny finally floated down and then dropped, he meant a smoke! Why not, when in Rome and all that.

Out came the Kenwood blender, where else would you keep the naughty stuff. After a few minutes whisking, the dry green leaves were now finely chopped and our host, who had obviously indulged before rolled - rather expertly I thought - two large joints. (In today's vernacular spliffs or reefers.)

The rest of the evening is somewhat blurred and not just because this happened forty years ago. However, I do recall someone suggesting we take in the view from the roof. Our host was the assistant manager of the hotel and consequently had the keys. (notice keys, not codes this is the pre-digital era) With one joint down and well into our second why not take in the view from the eleventh-floor roof of a major hotel. Health and safety hadn't even been conceived back then so the waist high rail around the edge was a useful, guide to where the roof ended, and gravity takes over.

Clouds of green and blue smoke formed over our heads and then floated away into the Caribbean, where any early morning fishermen would be guaranteed to be stoned later that day.

Also, as I discovered later, the ventilation shaft for the air conditioning was located on the roof and several guests had been misdiagnosed later that morning as having had too much to drink! The intoxicating smell of the weed must have been dragged down the air ducks and into the bar area where several late-night drinkers had a free dose of Ocho Rios best.

So, my story is short because time and the weed have dulled the memory. However, I can't look at a Kenwood mixer these days without getting the shakes.

2. "Show me the Money"

Location: The Ocean road near Boscobel Aerodrome, Ocho Rios in the parish of St Marys, Middlesex County, Jamaica. 1974.
Time: approx. 4.30pm

You know that feeling when driving a car and you arrive at your destination only to wonder what happened to the twenty or so minutes it took to get there?

Well I was in that 'dead time' when my senses heard and caught sight of blue and white flashing lights and what was of course, a police car, occupying my rear-view mirror.

I had just finished a meeting with the members of St Marys Parish Council on the North Coast and felt I had done well on my first solo outing.

Here's a warning sign, never start self-congratulations until you are safely back at base with a rum and coke to hand. Me, my files and twelve members of the council including the mayor had completed a half year review of their insurance arrangements.

There had even been some laughter as I unsuccessfully tried to reply to a question in the local Jamaican patwa, much to the amusement and desk banking of the Fire Chief. One of his prized engines was off the road for repairs following an accident and he was keen to have it back in action, hence his support for me. Others including the mayor were equally amused and the sight of twelve local politicians and me in such light-hearted spirits was something I could never have imagined a year ago in rainy Manchester.

There in the old court room the mayor brought proceedings to a finish and banged his gavel hard on the desk followed by, "de meeting closed."

So that's where I had been for the past twenty minutes of my drive, day dreaming of my success, however that was about to end, as I was instructed to "pull over." I dutifully complied bringing my new white Avenger, with six extra spot lights, to a halt. Due to the lack of street lighting along the coast road, I had been advised to have this extra lighting fitted, great for me but not so for occupants of oncoming traffic.

Now, parked behind me was a black and white Dodge police car, like the ones in American movies (circa 1975). A very tall man exited from the passenger side, navy blue trousers with a red stripe running down the outside of each leg, light blue shirt well decorated with badges some metal and others sewn into the shirt like a boy scout, for achieving certain skills and a top pocket full of pens. To complete the apparition, he wore a blue flat cap with a red trim again very influenced by the American versions.

Finally, the heavy armour, a black belt that supported handcuffs, various other objects and of course his revolver, just the one.

I wound down my window - no electrics, all manual back then, to hear, "Stay in de car man," followed by, "You know why wi stop ya?"

Nothing came out, my eye line was stuck on his revolver, not waiting for a reply, he continued, "You was speedin, show me your licence."

I hand he, who has the gun, my official document.

"What Diz"? he asks.

"Diz?" I repeat not understanding.

"Diz," he repeats holding my UK driving licence.

"Dis my," I start and then quickly change to, "This is my UK licence officer."

He replied, "Me no seen one like Dis (here we go again) before, I has to check it out, wait dare."

With that he returns to consult with his mate in the black and white.

Bottom line is I now have a ticket for speeding and as it appears on the summons '**you must appear in person at court, one week from today [date specified] at the council chambers in the parish of St Mary, County of Middlesex'.**

Judgement day, and I have been advised by other ex-pats to arrive early and take lots of dollars, the amount of the fine being unspecified. The fine is payable immediately i.e. before you leave the court house or as it states on the monopoly board 'go straight to jail.' And there you sit until a kindly soul pays your fine.

Consequently, I am on time and loaded with $300 Jamaican dollars, a princely sum then, representing 5% of my annual pay in 1974.

By the way, the court room is the very same room in which I held that successful meeting the week before.

My offence number and name are called and up I go into the box marked 'accused,' just like the one at the Old Bailey. The bailiff reads out: "**Case number 4. Lowe. ef, speedin your onour**".

Across the court from me, sitting on the judge's bench are three very familiar faces. It's the mayor, head judge, well he would be and two of the other councillors from last week's meeting all grinning through pearly white teeth.

They recognise me!

From somewhere I hear a voice,"How you plead"?

He's talking to me, it's hot, I'm perspiring and in a room with some sixty other people comprising of defendants, court officials, police officers and the masses in the public gallery. Everyone seems to be talking at once, no 'silence in court,' here it's a free-for-all like the trading floor at the Wall Street Stock Exchange.

To make matters worse, no deodorant on earth could mask the presence of this human body odour, whenever there is a breeze from the open windows a full dose of this human perfume is propelled around the room.

The sun is blasting through the window blinds, the fans are on full alert and I am stood there in full suit, shirt and tie. Everyone else is cool, shorts open neck shirts (before they became fashionable) you name it and its acceptable, but a suit, I ask you!

Throw yourself at the mercy of the court my friends had told me, so I do.

In answer to the question posed by the bailiff, I plead:

"Guilty your honour," and I should have stopped right there, but no, I continued. "I would like to register my apologies to the court and the police officers for this offence, any inconvenience and wasting your and their time"

Judge number two shouts, "Guilty fine $300."

The Mayor who clearly remembers me and why wouldn't you the only man in a suit, smiles and comments, "You no waste our time man, we just made tree hundred dollar!" Hilarious.

With that the whole court room burst into uncontrollable laughter. Jamaicans have an acute sense of humour, the judge's comment has ignited the congregation into a hysterical mob, even the judge is suppressing a smile.

As I am leaving the accounts dept., having relieved myself of $300 and now almost bankrupt, I hear the words, "Jail" from the court room. There's a poor soul who will be seeing bars tonight, and not the ones you can order a drink at.

Using his gavel, the judge quietens the room ready for the next contestant in **"Show me the money or head straight to Jail".**

My fine, one of these times 60!

Book Eleven - What Next?

1. Pedestrians Environmental Act (PEA) 2019

So far this morning I have witnessed two near misses and one head on collision.

Fortunately, in the latter event there were no fatalities nor were the emergency services required, damage was limited to the loss of a freshly brewed cup of latte' and the soaking of a shearling coat (retail £3,000) on which the entire contents of the coffee were distributed.

Neither of the parties, both female, were injured although pride was at stake and a few harsh words were exchanged. The younger, in a broad scouse accent and a mature lady from Cheshire both using the same expletives, however the latter delivered in a more eloquent manner.

The incident, which is becoming common place occurred on the pavement directly outside my coffee shop of choice on London Road Alderley Edge.

So, to recap, picture this, the scouse exits the shop holding coffee cup in one hand, her mobile phone in the other and in deep conversation with her mate Talula. Equally oblivious of the impending doom is dog lady, head down and talking to her two Labradoodles both pulling her forward, at pace on separate leads.

That's the scene in front of me.

Seconds later scouse walks into dog lady who receives an unwanted coffee shower, mobile phone goes skywards landing on London Road and is immediately squashed under the wheels of a car with T-Mobile logos on the sides, how ironic is that! The Labradoodles literally go barking mad attacking innocent passers-by, customers inside the coffee shop are entertained as a heated argument ensues, with accusations flying back and forth.

This gets me thinking, is it time for the Road Traffic Act of 1930 to be extended and cover pedestrian movement on streets and pavements. Let's call it the Pedestrian Environmental Act 2019 or PEA for short.

Imagine, in the incident described above, the police and an ambulance are called, as well as the RSPCA to cater for the traumatised Labradoodles. Names and addresses are exchanged, and the police cordon off the pavement area as a crime scene. Claim and counter claim are made for personal injury, damage to clothing and loss of earnings due to time off work through stress. Also, would this involve a court case? If so, I may be called as a witness to the 'incident'.

This would make excellent material for Peter Kay to make a new mini-series or Netflix might issue a box set on sale at Christmas.

The introduction of the PEA would require pedestrians to hold a valid licence to use the pavement/street areas, children under six are issued with a provisional and must be accompanied by an adult. Those over age 60 would need a medical MOT every year and of course insurance for third party or fully comprehensive cover.

Now for the near misses I mentioned at the beginning. The first involves the terror of most pedestrians, the street jogger. They weave in and out of walkers until, on this occasion when a mother with pram must brake as jogger, to use motor speak, "cuts her up". Basically, overtaking and then suddenly darting back in front of pram thereby causing mum to do an emergency stop.

This is an example of speeding and dangerous running, which if it involved a motor vehicle would carry a sentence of six points on the driver's licence, plus a fine or a twelve-month driving ban.

Under the new PEA the jogger would receive a lifelong ban from using the pavement and confiscation of his Nike running shoes and lycra shorts. *Sec 23 sub 4. Of the Act. No athletic activities allowed on pavement or street areas.*

She, the mother may have suffered whiplash through braking so hard, necessitating a neck brace and the baby might need counselling in later life for PTSD.

Under the PSA the use of bicycles on pavements would not be permitted and those in charge of a pram or similar buggy would need the advanced heavy-duty licence. Sec 6 b of the new Act. *(Applicable to those with four wheels or more, excluding supermarket trolleys, provided they are restricted to the carpark).* For activities undertaken by ramblers, hikers, mountaineers and general off-road walking they would be exempt. Sec 8 of the Act.

A slow lane would be introduced for the users of zimmer frames or walking sticks. Occasionally when there is heavy congestion on the pavements, we might have to introduce single file walking and movement in pairs or 'tandoming' as it has become known would be banned.

No stopping on street corners for a chat either - that might cause congestion or an accident - resulting in a one-off penalty charge for unauthorised parking of oneself. *(Sec 12. Para 2 sub 2.)*

Pedestrians who are caught the worse for wear from drink or other substances; this would be classified as an offence. They would be arrested and placed in a cooling off centre overnight, the next day charged with 'drunk in charge of self'. *(Sec 3d of the Act).*

Those non-joggers caught running, would be issued a speeding ticket with the possibility of points on their licence for 'walking without due care and attention' or 'dangerous walking', the latter resulting in an automatic ban or custodial sentence.

All pedestrians would have to pass the pavement-users test, both practical involving an emergency stop and written paper before being issued with the appropriate licence. Insurance would be mandatory. Obviously, there would be costs involved, not least of which who would police these activities? Funds would be available from licencing, medicals for over 60's, fines and the insurance industry would have to provide cover at a reasonable premium where the government would charge insurance tax, as they do at present.

Head cameras for pedestrians, similar to those now worn by cyclists are optional, however recommended. These would provide vital evidence in the event of an incident to determine liability and insurers were offering discounted premiums for those who wore the cameras.

This is a whole new world of bureaucracy, creating many new jobs in administration and a new position of 'Street Officers' for - pavement patrol - from whom the Inland Revenue would collect income tax and NIS contributions.

However, these extra rules may deter some people from venturing out, resulting in an explosion of on-line shopping and home deliveries via drones. The result, less people on the streets so reducing congestion and fewer accidents.

The second near miss incident involved two people both on their mobile phones and unaware they were walking directly towards each other. Until, at the last second, prior to impact, one finishes his call and looks up, swerving he narrowly avoids the other party who is still locked in his own world, listening to a recording telling him, *"your call is important to us please hold."*

Had they been caught, then under the new PEA both would have received a six-point penalty on their licence and banned from using mobiles for 12 months. *(Sec 2 of the Act. Using a phone whilst in control of oneself).*

Could it work?

Not a cat in hell's chance.

However, you never know with this bunch of so-called politicians we have these days, if it's a money spinner then they may consider this new act. If so then they didn't get the idea from me!

2. Consent.

Harvey Weinstein and Kevin Spacy; it all kicked off with these two guys in the 2000's. The newspapers were full of revelations about unwanted attention from men towards women. New claims - some going back years - were aired daily against Politicians, Actors and TV personalities, they had all been at it. So, a new Act of Parliament was introduced called the 'Consent Act' of 2022.

Now a written form or e-version of consent is required from any two people wishing to communicate or what is more to the point make actual bodily contact with each other in either a public or private place. Initially, it was designed to protect females from such unsolicited attention from male predators.

However, the #metoo brigade had their way, and the Act has been extended over the years to cover, what we previously regarded as innocent socialising, in public places, at leisure and in the work place. Consequently, the effect of these restrictions and bureaucracy has resulted in the country almost grinding to a halt.

In the process the population of the UK is in its 10th year of decline. Maternity wards are closing, and midwifery is almost finished as a profession. From a near 70 million high in 2018 we are now at an all-time low of 23 million in 2055, with the extinction of the human race predicted around 2084. Also, net Immigration was amongst the contributing factors partly following the UK's final exit from the EU in 2025.

Against this background I enter the previously free and relaxing atmosphere of my local coffee shop.

Once strangers would complement owners on their doodle dogs in the shop. Dog owners would congregate and while away the time in canine talk, or pat babies on the head and exchange stories of what the little darlings had been up to that day, ranging from the effects of crupe, teething or driving *grandma nuts.

Occasionally the decibel levels would go through the roof, as one little cherub objected to being ignored, with a screaming fit worthy of an honour's degree.

Some customers were known to share a table when the place was busy, engage in conversation, exchange newspapers and generally bump along together. Even on occasions saying "goodbye" when leaving the shop or adding, "hope to see you again soon," without any hidden agenda, just being sociable.

All that changed when the #metoo movement took hold with a variety of splinter groups, you name it and they formed a movement and complained of discrimination, sexism, every ism under the sun.

It only takes one objector and a whole nation must change its buying habits. Take Kleenex tissues as an example. One female objector and the whole packaging is changed to avoid using the words 'Man Size'.

Next, an article in the daily papers condemning the departed Walt Disney for his adaptation of Snow White. (originally published in Grimms Fairy Tales in 1812 as *SchneeweiBchen*). Prince charming, a male, pecks this *bird on the cheek to awaken her from a coma-induced sleep perpetrated by the evil Queen. He is accused of an unsolicited attack on her person and branded a rapist. Then to cap it all he is placed on the sex offenders register. Poor guy thought he was doing her a favour.

According to the new Act he should have asked for her permission - don't forget she's in a coma - or that of a near relative, who were probably the seven dwarfs, sorry vertically challenged uncles.

So, back to the day when I enter the café and reach for my mobile and engage the 'Consent App'. This is now a must do for anyone entering a public place such as restaurants, café's, libraries etc. I start to fill in the questionnaire as follows.

Do you consent to the following?
Q1. A conversation with the barista?

A. Yes. (otherwise I can't order my drink you numpty), is what I feel like saying.

Q2. A conversation with dog owners, parents, small children?

A. NO, under no circumstances.

Q3. In the event of illness would you consent to mouth to mouth resuscitation from all, some or none of the following? Male, female, LGBT or other (specify)

A. Just do it!

Q4. Are you willing to use newspapers and other reading material that may have been handled by earlier patrons?

A. YES, I like to read the 'who's no longer with us' column in the Times.

Q5. Will you need to use the bathroom during your stay? If so, please bear in mind this equipment may have been used by other patrons recently.

A. Possibly. (How the hell do I know if my prostate and bladder will cope)? Is what I am tempted to answer.

Next on my screen I see the green light, I have been accepted and must abide by the 'no contact rules' I have chosen.

The whole population of the UK are now on the NCR, (National Consent Register), a bit like the Domesday Book of 1086. Anyone with a previous conviction under the Consent Act trying to enter a public place, after completing this form, will trigger alarm bells. Thereby alerting everyone that a convicted handshaker, unwanted talker, patter on the back, man hugger is at large.

The other contentious issue that emerged around that time [2020] related to double standards. Example:

No one objects when David Gandy or Beckham appear in adverts exposing their conkers to the world at large. Yet Bunny girls, motor racing cheer leaders and other scantily clad promotional gals are frowned upon. Also, let's not forget the so-called celebs who virtually bare all when on the red carpet at the *OSCARS, BAFTAS* or other such luvie gatherings.

What would the likes of Emily Davidson - who famously threw herself in front of the King's horse Anmer during the Derby of 1913 - have made of today's female generation? It all seems to be heading in one direction and I don't mean the dotty boy's band.

George Orwell was well ahead of his time with the novel *1984*, the only difference, instead of Big Brother looking over your shoulder its now Big Sister, you have been warned!

End.

Note. Some of the terminology may be considered politically incorrect or inappropriate. However, the author considered this essential to the story line. Happy days!

3. Top Cat

It came as no surprise that Purple Velvet (PV) arrived late for her lunch appointment at the Half Mile Tower, such was her habit. Although it took two minutes to reach the restaurant on the 407th floor, she preferred the old lotus lift of 2019 to the modern hover taxi, which gives me the opportunity to provide you with more information about Purple.

PV owns the Half Mile Tower along with the restaurant on the top floor, which she inherited from her grandfather, Rue' Costa, following his unexplained suicide last year in 2059. In addition, she was the sole beneficiary of the last remaining quantity of pure Columbian Coffee beans - some forty kilos - that Rue' had stashed away following the extinction of the bean in 2050. A deadly disease hit the fertile areas in South America and Sri Lanka wiping out the world's crops and seedlings.

Sensing a business opportunity, she opened a retro coffee shop on the top floor and those that could afford it (coffee) would continue to participate in their drug of choice, from latte and cappuccino to the newly designed 'Bulgarian Bomber'. It [the shop] was decorated in the style of 2019 - when the consumption of coffee was at its height - with natural wood tables, disposable cups before they were banned and leather chairs. Although the latter had to be replaced with simulated leather following a ban in the late twenties on animal skins used on furniture. Her final touch was the introduction of Baristas, dressed in black T-shirts with the Tower Coffee logo [TC] emblazoned on the front in gold lettering.

She's arrived at floor 407, so to continue.

Lift doors open and out she walks onto the heavy marble floor of the restaurant roof garden and there on display are the only remaining coffee plants in the world protected by bullet proof glass.

She is here to meet her number one clone, of which she has three. The latest 'must have' for the up and coming zillionaire of the 60's is no longer an original Beatle's jacket or latest smart phone, but a clone of oneself.

The craze took hold and those with the finance were able to clone as many of themselves as they wanted. Clones rapidly became big business allowing one to rent or lease selfies to third parties for set periods at a substantial premium.

Back at the dining table JV ordered her favourite coffee from a waiter, the George Clooney clone. She now had several of these male clones and Clooney along with Hew Edwards the Barista, were her favourites. With the near extinction of the coffee bean, she was able to charge whatever extortionate fee she wanted and today the going rate to clients was $3000 per serving. To her it was a free luxury, however her 'number one' had to be satisfied with water. Not to be wasted on clones was this liquid gold.

She was in high spirits after securing the lease on a Beckham number fourteen - from a limited edition of twenty-five - for a three-year period. It was the thirty-year-old Becks version and the costs were slightly offset after trading in the now older Tom Cruise (pre-scientology) number six, again from a limited edition.

The Clone Leasing Programme (CLP) had become quite a money spinner for the celebs with many cashing in on their looks and fame. Although the Victoria Beckham smiling version was still a rarity. Also, there had been a number of high-profile failures, the David Gandy and Idris Elber clones were thought to be good sellers however, there were several left, even after the Black Monday and Christmas sales of 2059. So, production ceased when Gandy lost the M&S contract and Idris was overlooked for the Bond movies.

Also, on decline were the rentals of Fiona Bruce after her appearance on Any Questions. She was considered to be far too intelligent and prone to in-depth debate. The guys leasing her obviously wanted a quiet life, consequently many were returned even though the agreements made no provision for refunds.

On the plus side, Clones of Mary Berry and Delia Smith were a roaring success and with the number limited to fifty each, expensive. The one-year term with an option for a further two years seemed the most popular. It was thought their prowess in the kitchen was the motivating factor behind their popularity.

Problems started to appear about five years in to the scheme when most of the clone agreements expired. There was simply no market for returns with people wanting the latest version of pop star, film goddess or sports person. So, what was to be done with them? The Daily Mail ran an article - like that on plastics in the twenties - on "What to do with your unwanted clones?" One couldn't just kill them off, although several tried and court cases of clonicide were pending.

There were other issues too, including reports of an incident involving a football team consisting of all David Beckham clones. In the second half the referee had to send off one player, however, he didn't know which Beckham had committed the foul and no one owned up, so the match was abandoned.

In another case several diners at a well-known restaurant had Daniel Craig (James Bond) clones as their escorts. At some point in the evening an argument ensued between Bond and Bond which had to be broken up by Bond and another Bond. Confusion reigned, and the police ended up arresting Bond, Bond, Bond and yes Bond.

Due to excessive cloning over the years, DNA patterns had changed and certain genes had ceased to exist. This was discovered by the CLP who found the compassionate gene resistant to transfer from the original. Consequently, hundreds of females were disappointed with their Becks, Gandy and Craig clones who were now non-responsive to their affections. Hearts were broken, and numerous returns were made.

Meanwhile back on the 407th floor of Half Mile Tower JV and the clone were in deep conversation. In one movement JV stood up from the table walked to the safety rail and launched herself off into space.

Unsurprisingly it took less time for her to reach the bottom than when she had taken the lift in the opposite direction earlier that day. JV now occupied most of the heliport parking area on the ground floor.

Back on floor 407 clone 'number one' moved to the chair previously occupied by JV. A rather thin smile emerged across her face, the compassionate gene may have ceased to exist however, greed and jealousy, the ugly side of humans, was starting to grow in number one, now Top Cat!

At the autopsy the pathologist had very little to work on, JV having spread herself thinly over the ground. However, part of the stomach remained intact, revealing the contents, nothing more sinister than coffee.

What followed over the next few weeks was an alarming number of suicides all of whom were equally puréed. Eventually a common factor emerged when the authorities established the victims had dined at the Half Mile Restaurant and traces of coffee were also found during the autopsies.

On exhuming the body of her grandfather, Rue' Costa it revealed he also had similar traces of coffee in his remains. The old man had been secretly filtering the deadly beans and unknowingly drinking himself to suicide.

Further analysis on the remaining stash of coffee that JV had inherited, found traces of the deadly virus that had eradicated the bean all those years ago.

Paranoia set in as people started to question who was the original and who was the clone. Hilarious, yet weird scenes were played out in court at the Old Baily where Delia accused Delia of being a clone and called the other forty-nine Delias as witnesses. This got even more bizarre when legal counsel questioned the originality of the Judge.

To sum up, the DNA was the same excepting that greed and jealousy had replaced compassion. So, what's new there, you may ask? and exactly what did number one say to JV that made her go skydiving, without a parachute?

In 2065 cloning was universally banned however, by then no one knew how many roamed the earth. Meghan and Harry were turning up everywhere, the Donald had managed to be re-elected President for a tenth time and Aguero was still scoring goals for MCFC.

To say people viewed each other with a degree of suspicion is putting it mildly. So, my advice to you is, when next you meet a familiar face be careful of the conversation, stay away from high buildings and stick to water.

4. Kendal Milne.

Location: Manchester
Year: 2150

Is this a dream? Have I just woken up? Is this real?

Look, it's your story so you can make it what you want, stop messing around and set the scene. Although, whether it makes any sense or not is up to the reader.

OK, I'm in apartment five on the third floor of what I understand used to be the Kendal Milne Department store on Deansgate Manchester way back in the 1900's. From my bedroom window, at the rear of the building, I look out over something that used to be called a multi-storey car park, now block number two and full of similar apartments to mine.

Front facing locations are slightly more expensive having a great view over the water and height. The old lifts are still in use and the original ground to roof green granite staircase is now an art gallery, they had to keep it for health and safety, a throwback to when people weren't responsible for their own actions and litigation was rampant.

This morning I have an appointment with the 'Genetics Overseers Department' or GOD for short, to review my mortality rating. The regulations have changed, previously the automatic termination clause would apply on reaching age 70. However now, one can elect for euthanasia at either age 60 or 65 and get increased benefits and various discounts, as an incentive for taking the early options. Otherwise the automatic termination clause kicks in.

At the last election, offering this choice was a vote winner for Corbyn the third. It allows me discounted rates on orders from IKEA, pizza express and at the gym on the second floor of my building known as *CORBYN CONDOS*. Although some comedian has climbed the front of the building and sprayed a letter *M* between the *O* and *S*.

Violation of state property will incur a five-year deduction from his or her mortality rating if they are caught, as I am sure they will under our, zero tolerance policy. All hail the Corbyn.

Leaving my apartment, I head for the public prosecco fountain, one no longer needs a prescription and it's much easier to obtain now they have abolished the previous class A drug rating. However, there is a queue and it will involve a long wait, never mind there will be several other fountains on the way to the clinic.

Anyhow my appointment was successful, and I decided to opt for the age 65 termination package, so my wrist band now has a bar code scheduled to expire on 1st of January in 2150, my 65th birthday, provided I don't incur any violation debits. No worries that's 25 years off and anything can happen. On arriving home, I make my way to the roof and the drone port where the deliveries arrive, this week from Aldi and Beckhams Bargains.

Motor vehicles of all types have disappeared since the oil ran out and electric cars were consuming too much electricity, so they were banned. However, following advances in Artificial Intelligence and the drone deliveries, travel has become unnecessary now. 'Drones are Us' can deliver whatever you want, and holidays are available via virtual reality, just plug in and choose your destination.

This year I went to the Hotel Arctic, where I believe the temperatures used to be around minus 70 degrees. However, since the global warming it's now the hottest place on the planet, the sun having changed orbit so that the Sahara Desert is now a ski resort.

Here in Manchester we had roads, now it's the river Deansgate with a jet ski park in St Anns's Marina. The tourist websites describe Manchester as the Modern Venice, whatever Venice was?

No one took the threat of global warming seriously enough until 2056 when the ice caps, North and South, collapsed, melted and millions were drowned. Apart from the new ski resorts in Angola and Zambia the continent of African no longer exists. Also, Russia caught the floods consequently no more cold war. If anything, what's left of that country is now an exclusive summer resort in Siberia for the super-rich. All the Oligarchs lost their money when the oil dried up and had to sell their yachts and Chelsea FC.

Once the floods started, 'height' became the currency on which property values were based. No longer square footage when buying a house, it's now all about how high the property is above water level. Most of the department stores converted to self-contained flats on the top floors with a restaurant and gymnasium at the water level, previously known as the ground floor. M&S made a killing with their high street stores, however previous property hot spots plummeted in value with those that could afford it moving to the 10th floor of the Deansgate Tower on the river Deansgate.

Alderley Edge for example is now a swamp, generally regarded as a no-go area although I believe they still have a local Costa and Nero coffee bars floating on the London Road River bank.

The floods destroyed those parts of the USA where wheat was grown, and huge herds of cattle were wiped out in the US and South America. Sheep farming in Australia is now extinct with only 20% of the original landmass surviving, the capital having moved to Aires Rock.

So, with the food chain under threat and the world population cut by a half the governments of those countries still in existence made a joint decision, not to limit birth control but introduce a termination policy. Thereby ensuring a younger and controlled population which would not place too much of a burden on our limited resources.

For sports we go to the old football stadiums, of those that are left. The Etihad is now the home of the Manchester White Bates water polo team. There was another ground somewhere in Salford however, it didn't stand the test of time, apparently it was built on foundations of sand and crumbled when under attack.

Must go now I'm expecting a hologram visit from my great grandparents, they're both 200 years old and as they survived the global warming are exempt from the termination regs. They don't get out much, although gran still looks good must have been that stuff they used in the early 2000, Botox or something.

Now you just nip into a branch of 'Looking Glass' and have a face transplant. When you're tired of that look then trade it in for a newer one, provided you maintain your direct debit, you're OK.

Otherwise it's repossession and you end up with your original one. Which after fifty years of aging can be quite a shock meeting your previously unseen aged self.

5. Antique Roadshow - 2037

Here's a new item for antiques roadshow, 'Facelifts'.

How would that work I wonder, how old is the facelift or the person?

Was it done by a well-known, now deceased plastic surgeon, that might add value?

Why stop there, what about female rear-end enhancements and other parts of the male anatomy?

Also, Botox injections, have any lasted the test of time, if so do they have a value? it's a whole new show for the future.

My mind wonders. It's the year 2037 and I'm at the Antiques Road Show: A young girl pushes a wheel chair containing occupant towards Fion, the presenter. *"Hi this is the facelift that my grandma had done in 1999, looks good and she's still wearing it although she did pass away in 2012".*

The Expert considers grannie, *"How did you come by her"?*

Young girl answers, *"She used to belong to my mother, however, they had nowhere to keep her, so she gave her to me on my 21st birthday"*

He continues: *"It's definitely an original, slight crustation around the neck, which one would expect after all this time, and the knife work is excellent, you can hardly see the join. I have seen other work by the same surgeon, however, that was a simple nose and tuck job. He's a very sort-after guy and these early 'full lifts' are very collectable."*

"If she were to go to auction today, I would have to value her at…" He mentions a figure.

The surrounding crowd gasp at the valuation, then granddaughter states, *"That's wonderful but we'll never sell her."*

Fion turns to camera. Without a frown in sight, a fixed smile and hardly moving her lips, *"Join us next week when we will be in Birmingham asking",*

"Have you got a grannie in the attic"?

6. Auto clinics - 2050

Changes within the NHS started back in 2016 when they introduced the auto blood pressure machine at the surgery in Chelford. A simple device with a sleeve, pop your arm in and wait for pressure to build, after a few seconds you are issued with a ticket showing *SYS 165, DIA 62 and PUL 59* or something similar.

So, what does that mean? Consult the chart and its abnormal, must make appointment to see the doctor.

It [the sleeve] was supposed to free up more time for the doctors and whilst initially it was considered a success and a daily ritual for locals, it has become counterproductive. Once the novelty wore off it resulted in more appointments with the GP when patients, now known as clients, had an above average reading and wanted to check with their GP if there was a problem. Queues began to form at the 'sleeve' as clients took several readings one after the other then tried to work out the mean average.

Also, appointments with doctors were becoming more difficult to arrange with long waiting times. So, the more clued-in clients began to block-book two months ahead, just in case they had contracted an illness or injury by that time.

Since then there have been numerous changes over the past 34 years and particularly following the great flu epidemic of 2025. Because of that outbreak the NHS accelerated their research and found a cure for the common cold. Who would have thought a dose of marmite twice a week and that's it, job done. Shares in Marmite go through the roof.

This however, had its drawbacks, as those people who were allergic to marmite had a negative reaction, So, since the common cold was irradiated, *marmititus* was introduced to the Concise Oxford English Dictionary. i.e. *(entry: a severe reaction to the substance marmite, recommended cure, do not eat marmite!)*

Now, we have both the 'Drive through' clinic which can be found at MacDonalds and the local 'Auto surgery' which Tesco are considering installing these in their bigger stores.

Today, 1st October 2044 we are at the local Auto clinic in Macclesfield. In some ways they resemble laundrettes with a bank of sleeves or portals instead of washing machines, along one wall. Clients sit one behind the other with their arm resting in one of these sleeves, then enter your pin number, name and date of birth. Each sleeve has a specific purpose. There's the one for blood tests, just a little scratch and the needle has done its job. Others are programmed to instantly provide a diagnosis, work out what medication you need and then, hey presto! in goes another needle and you now have a vein full of meds.

Pills went out of fashion decades ago, so whether its measles or appendicitis you name it and you get one shot per month. That's if you're treated by the NHS, go privately and you can have as many as you need provided you remain financially viable.

Cuts and bruises are dealt with by the laser skin grafter in booth number three. The robot arm takes a thin slice of skin from your most meaty part and then transfers this to the area to be treated. A shot of the new marmite-based antibiotics in the rear and you are done for a month.

Here's Joe, for his monthly check up, let's listen in as he is greeted by the attendant, who looks quite natty in his florescent health and safety jacket. By the way there are no more nurses, they all moved abroad.

"Haemorrhoids again Joe?" asked the attendant and then continued, *"Back to the wall please against the rectum meter, you'll feel a little prick and yes all done, you can pull your pants up now."*

The maternity booths, with a sign on the door "Pregnantees', are in the next room. Since 2045 when legislation was introduced to ensure there was no discrimination, Men, Us's, LGBT's and other groups were given the marmite-based womb pill thus allowing them to conceive. Don't ask!

The authorities had to drop the term pregnancy, which was considered elitist relating only to women, as per the 2016 definition. Hence the term 'Pregnantees' was born, no pun intended.

Doctors have now accelerated the incubation period from nine months down to two weeks. This resulted in a huge saving to the NHS who can now predict the exact time and day of delivery. Consequently, one can choose a home, work or clinic delivery and within minutes continue with one's daily routine be that work, at the gym, coffee shop or on holiday overseas. Since the fourteenth Brexit referendum of 2045, EU countries now offer similar facilities to those mention above, provided one holds an EU-Brexit medical card with the 'pregnantee' extension.

For emergencies, serious accidents or illness there is the NHS drone ranger, offering a collection and patient delivery service. Although presently there is a three-hour delay in response time, Fedex have their own fleet of drones and offer an immediate collection.

Following a proliferation in the use of these drones, the limitations on air space and landing slots, we have seen an increase of mid-air collisions. Patients were literally left hanging around waiting for controllers to disentangle the offending drones. Consequently, all drone traffic in the area had to be diverted leading to congestion on alternative flight paths. Like the motorway congestions of the late 20th Century, before they became obsolete.

Consequently, the NHS are commandeering Ambulances from motor museums. These are described as a land based motorised vehicle, used extensively in the early 2000's to convey patients to hospitals, with a human crew of two, who were known as medics.

They (the ambulances) have been converted from the old petrol driven to an electrically powered system. The only delay now is finding mechanics who have the knowledge of these vintage forms of transport, people who know how to drive them and a supply of rubber tyres.

To accommodate these vehicles the government are opening the previously abandoned old motorway system, starting with the M6, M1 and M25.

The RAC and AA are recruiting!

Nearly the end.

You may be wondering what the answer was to the chapter 'What's in a name'? There were four options.

The answer: -

The barista walks to the delivery point and shouts "Costa". No one batted an eye lid, the conversations never missed a beat, the crowd just carried on at high volume. Answer C.

So, my little experiment had failed, however there's always a next time and another Coffee company at which to test my experiment.

Baristas beware.

Now it's the end, thanks for reading.